Musical Theatre

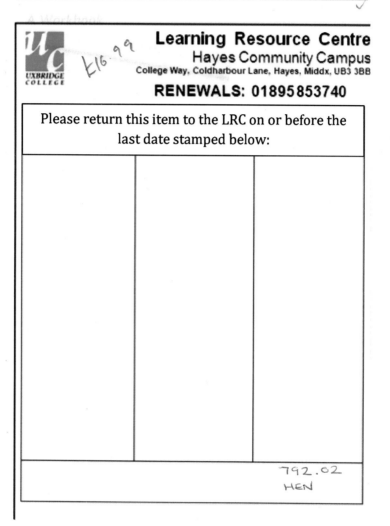

Musical Theatre

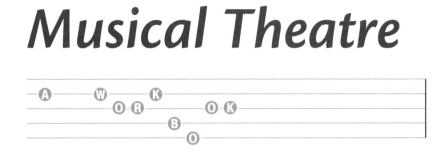

A WORKBOOK

David Henson and Kenneth Pickering

palgrave
macmillan

First published 2013 by
PALGRAVE MACMILLAN

Palgrave Macmillan in the UK is an imprint of Macmillan Publishers Limited, registered in England, company number 785998, of Houndmills, Basingstoke, Hampshire RG21 6XS.

Palgrave Macmillan in the US is a division of St Martin's Press LLC, 175 Fifth Avenue, New York, NY 10010.

Palgrave Macmillan is the global academic imprint of the above companies and has companies and representatives throughout the world.

Palgrave® and Macmillan® are registered trademarks in the United States, the United Kingdom, Europe and other countries.

ISBN 978–1–137–33162–5

This book is printed on paper suitable for recycling and made from fully managed and sustained forest sources. Logging, pulping and manufacturing processes are expected to conform to the environmental regulations of the country of origin.

A catalogue record for this book is available from the British Library.

A catalog record for this book is available from the Library of Congress.

Printed in China

Contents

Part 3 Understanding the Musical 71

5 The Anatomy of the Musical 73

6 The Origins and Development of Musical Theatre 85

Figures

Acknowledgements

The authors wish to express their gratitude to Marion Cox, for her imaginative illustrations; Alex Loveless, for his help and for permission to use his compositions; Kim Ismay, Irene Pickering and professors Kevin Landis and Joan Melton for their constructive criticism; colleagues and students at the universities of Kent and West London (London College of Music) for supporting our work; Charlotte Emmett, for her constant care in producing the typescript; and Jenni Burnell, our inspirational editor at Palgrave Macmillan.

Introduction: About This Book

Who is it for?

This workbook is intended primarily for **students** embarking on the study of Musical Theatre at college, at university or in a private studio. But it also provides help, ideas and guidance for **teachers** and **instructors**, who can adopt the book as a required or complementary text for courses of study.

What levels does it assume?

The workbook consists of material suitable for students on the first **two years** of degree or diploma courses or their equivalent. The authors appreciate that Musical Theatre may be studied as an aspect of Performing Arts, Dance or Theatre in a wide variety of contexts but the material offered in this workbook will be of value as a substantial introduction to this area of enquiry.

What previous experience is required?

We assume that you have probably gained entry to a course of study through an audition or a 'tryout' and have had some experience of taking part in or singing numbers from musicals. The precise prerequisites will vary from course to course but you will certainly need to bring a passion and enthusiasm for Musical Theatre to your work. Ideally, you should read music adequately or at least be able to demonstrate general musicianship. You should have a good ear for music and be reliable when working in a chorus or small ensemble. You do not need perfect pitch but you do need to realise that time is always precious in rehearsal and the repetitions of instructions for music, text or movement are not common. Accordingly, you need a quick mind and, at audition, to be able to answer simple questions relating to pitch and intonation. You may well be asked to sing simple melodic and rhythmic phrases, recognise major and minor chords and sing notes from within a chord played twice on a piano or respond to other simple aural exercises.

Additionally, you should be able to move well, learn and retain simple dance steps and read a dramatic text with understanding.

It is, of course, possible that you are coming to Musical Theatre for the first time, perhaps having enjoyed other aspects of theatre and now wanting to enhance your experience and skills. You may have simply been an enthusiastic audience member for shows but feel that you have the potential to become

1

involved in performance. Someone has noticed this potential and now you are feeling a little apprehensive: there is plenty in this workbook for you.

How we shall ask you to work

This book may be used as a basis for or supplement to a taught class in Musical Theatre **or** for private study.

In this workbook we want to enter into a dialogue with you by encouraging you to respond to various tasks and questions. We shall sometimes supply answers but at other times suggest sources for answers. The emphasis throughout is on learning through exploration and discovery and that is why it is a **work**book rather than a textbook.

The workbook is in **three parts**: in Parts **I** and **II** we provide activities and information intended to facilitate your **progressive mastery** of the **skills** of Musical Theatre. In **Part III** we offer activities and information designed to enhance your **understanding** of the whole field of Musical Theatre. **Part III** is specially designed so that it can be used **simultaneously** with Parts **I** and **II**.

How to use this workbook

There are as many ways of using this book as there are students and teachers who might have acquired it. Ideally, you should now **survey its entire contents** and then begin to work your way through **Part I**. However, because of your particular programme of study, needs or interests, you may find that there is material in Parts **II** and **III** that you can use at the same time. We assume a sense of progressive mastery but that may be achieved by the various routes that this book makes possible.

We would strongly recommend that you divide your time between acquiring the practical and artistic skills that form the contents of Parts I and II and the contextual and supporting material of Part III.

What if I cannot understand the terms being used?

In every learning situation, particularly in the rehearsal studio, you may hear other people using terms with which you are not familiar, and this may be embarrassing because you might think that you are the only person who does not understand. You may also feel that you do not fully understand the precise meaning of words used in this text or in other situations. We have provided a simple **glossary** to help you at the end of this workbook. If you are aware of unfamiliar words being used: (i) Look them up in the glossary and (ii) Make a note of them for your future use.

It is also possible that you feel baffled by all or some of the issues arising from reading a vocal score. We have provided a clear guide to this important aspect of your work in the form of a **Geographical Tour of a Vocal Score**. You will find this at the end of the book just after the **glossary**, and you should refer to it constantly if reading music presents a problem to you.

And a final thought to carry forward

We believe that one of the most misguided ideas of modern education is the labelling of young people as 'gifted and talented' and making special provision for them. In our view, everyone has gifts and talents, and it is our responsibility to nurture and develop them. You would not have been accepted as a student in this highly demanding and risky field had not somebody recognised that you have a gift and a talent: but that is only the beginning!

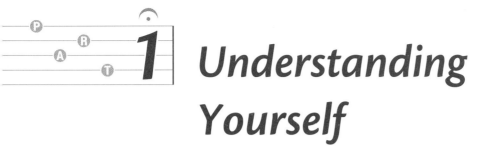

Understanding Yourself

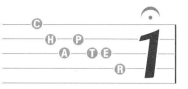

The Loneliness of the Young Actor-Singer in Training

Laying the foundations

The purpose of this book is to enable you to master the working practices associated with the study of Musical Theatre.

As a result you will be required to actively embrace the language of music and the music of language. In some ways, because of the nature of our existence and our means of everyday communication, our life's journey may prepare us to approach spoken text with more ease than the score and notation of the sung text. Our aim is to enable you to move easily between spoken and sung acting.

However good the quality of training and education you receive as an actor-singer, if your mind and body are not adequately prepared to acquire the necessary skills you will achieve little progress or sense of personal success, let alone gain the prospect of a performing career.

This book cannot replace a valuable and gifted teacher who inspires and encourages every action and observes and comments upon your progress. It can be used primarily for private study or as the basis for classes. Young actor-singers are not always provided with adequate tools to enable them to investigate the work prior to and during their advanced training, even if they have had many years of being involved in production work and/or study. Consequently, they may find the process of adjusting to full-time study a somewhat lonely experience.

Before we can begin to study the craft of performance and the intimate world of the actor-singer, we need to understand the world of the 'self' and perhaps even more importantly the relationship between the words we speak and self. If we are to be successful in a field where the playing out of truth is of utmost importance, then it is essential that each speaker should understand the nature of their own voice and their habitual patterns in order to identify other such patterns in the characters they may wish to play in their future performance career. We must understand the world of words and have humility and integrity in our investigation of language and action. We need to be able to interrogate every detail of the text and recognise the importance of the grammatical construction of each sentence. Yet we must also be able to explore aspects of our own physicality and develop these in a manner that reflects both the limitations and expectations of the character to be played.

Starting here. Starting now: Why am I here?

You may have been involved with this work for a long time in order to justify furthering your studies with the hope of entering the profession or you may have chosen to embark upon a subject which intrigues you.

So many journeys, influences, opportunities and life experiences bring us to the realisation that we have an ambition to study this area of work in a much more detailed manner. In the course of this search, you have undoubtedly been required to attend an audition and so have been tested in a thorough manner by those who are going to take on the responsibility of teaching you.

There will be many reasons why you and your fellow students were chosen and given a place on your course of study but you can be fairly certain that the one thing you all have in common is 'talent' – the one ingredient that cannot be taught!

The conclusion must be that all successful entrants to your course have different qualities and skills which now must be enhanced in order for the training to have some consistency and overall philosophy. It is in recognition of these varied experiences that this book reaches out to you all: to help and assist you in developing those areas that are, perhaps, not yet so developed. We hope that this book will contribute greatly to your style of study and provide you with strategies for acquiring skills that can promote your development as a performer. We aim to make your study and training an exciting time of realisation and personal growth.

Our basic premise is that you should now learn how to thoroughly embrace your skills. To scratch the surface is not sufficient: you must have the ability to maintain these skills and so develop them more strongly day by day.

Unfortunately, students sometimes are satisfied with success at a low level and never attempt to achieve more. Think about the training of athletes, who are always trying to surpass their previous personal record of achievement and success.

A new way of learning?

Up until this point in your education, most of your learning may have involved subjects where there is a clear 'right answer' or group of 'right answers' to a problem: now that you are embarking on the study of acting through singing – which is both an art form and a science – we need to embrace a new idea:

Paradox – *a seemingly contradictory statement that may nonetheless be true*

The nature of an art form is that much of it is **subjective** rather than **objective** and this certainly applies to singing. We all have different opinions as to what makes a 'good' sound. A Musical Theatre singer might be expected to sing everything from Gilbert and Sullivan to John Gay's *Beggar's Opera* or *Rock of Ages* and other contemporary shows, so there is a vast range of sounds and styles which can be considered to fall within the spectrum of Musical Theatre. There is a great scope for *paradox* within such a broad vocal church.

While we may not all agree on what makes a 'good' sound, or an 'attractive' sound, we are more likely to reach consensus on what is a 'safe' sound.

Richard Miller, the American voice scientist/pedagogue, once said to a group of young singers, 'every single singer has to make a choice: are you here for a good time or a long time?'

Our responsibility as teachers is to encourage all our students to sing in a way which will allow them to enjoy a lifetime of good vocal health. We are ethically bound to lead on the path of 'a long time' with your singing rather than encouraging or enabling you to choose the 'good time' route. The sounds that we encourage you to make may seem 'boring' or 'limited' based on what you hear on cast recordings or in live performance from some of your contemporaries; however, we demand that you trust that we are able to guide you towards a healthy long-term sustainable sound. If you choose to go off that path, to choose the 'good time' over the 'long time', then that is your choice, but you as the singer must accept the consequences of that decision.

During your training, you are likely to encounter ideas which seem to contradict each other. One teacher might tell you to pull in your stomach muscles, others might say to push them out, one might say to open your mouth two finger widths, while another says one finger width is optimal. **Don't be frustrated by this.** See that this can be the paradox of an art form. Your job as a student is to take each of these ideas **and try them out for yourself!** Singing is also a science, an active process, and can only be learned from actively trying ideas out in an experimental way. So don't dismiss any ideas even if they seem to contradict what you 'think' you know. Try it out for yourself and see how it fits your body and your voice.

We can't teach you how to sing – We can only give you the information. It is you who must teach yourself to sing

A recent theory has suggested that it takes 10,000 hours to master a skill. Based on our experience, this is probably true. If you are given 12 thirty-minute lessons per semester, then you have 12 hours of one-on-one vocal tuition over the course of the year. Over a three-year degree, you will receive 36 hours of one-on-one vocal tuition. As you can see, these 36 hours fall far short of the 10,000 hours required to master the skill of singing. So it is up to you to be putting in the daily practice, applying the learning from your various classes and teaching your body to respond to your thoughts/commands. It is your responsibility to take the information we give you and use it to teach yourself how to sing.

One final paradox: your voice needs to be regularly exercised but it also needs regular rest. You must work in a way which gives your voice both of these things. Only then can you grow.

A pause for reflection

Consider what is actually required of an actor-singer in the field of Musical Theatre and how these factors should impact upon strategies for supporting your study in a positive manner.

Dance	Music	Acting	Performance
movement	sing	speak	good level of fitness
dance patterns – memory	sight sing	sight read	confidence
awareness of dance styles	general musicianship	inflection and articulation	mental agility
memory	memory	memory	
repertoire	repertoire	repertoire	
inspirational role models	inspirational role models	inspirational role models	

Perhaps you are now feeling a little overwhelmed by the realisation that you are to be working in a field where you need expertise and skill in each of these areas in order to be successful.

Don't be daunted: just congratulate yourself that you have convinced others that you have the ability to work at your weaknesses in order to become the consummate performer. However, do make sure that you continue to maintain and develop your strengths further just like an athlete seeking to break his or her personal record.

You are not alone

In the first few weeks of your study, you will be faced with many decisions to make and skills to learn. How can we help you develop a method of training that allows you to work on your own and yet support the work required by your teachers?

We hope that by offering you practical ideas of how to prepare for class in all aspects of the Musical Theatre world, you will have an opportunity to match your other skills with ease and, thus, achieve your goals with growing confidence.

The direction of the following exercises will allow you to prepare adequately for any form of improvisation or preparatory acting/singing work that you may be required to embrace within your studies.

Most of us have a good control over our vocabulary and spoken voice and have acquired some useful skills when tackling the world of performance. The problems often occur when actors are then required to match these skills at the early stages of the training in terms of the sung voice.

In the primary stage of your training, you will probably be required to have a good idea about yourself and possess:

- A flexible and responsive voice (spoken/sung), body and mind free of tension and judgement.
- A good knowledge and awareness of the world around you and how these events and observations then colour personal judgements and influence the quality of thought and action. A system that enables your observations and personal reactions to be identified in detail.

- A clear understanding of what 'reality' and 'truth' are and how these impact upon your work as the actor-singer.
- A set of imaginative ideas (ingredients) that have been influenced and developed by the power of your observation.
- A sense of personal spontaneity.
- A truthful and meaningful relationship of self with events and actions to be played out.

Thinking about your 'self'

To establish some of these points you might like to investigate your awareness of self and so interrogate your own work and current position as a student within the field of Musical Theatre.

It is necessary to have a platform from which to jump, and if you are a little more critical of your own work and have identified the appropriate language and vocabulary of performance then the ability to take criticism from others becomes a less frightening and demoralising experience and can indeed become fun and a positive force in your development as an actor-singer.

The following questions, in relation to the sung and spoken voice and movement, are to encourage you to think about yourself in some detail and with precision. The questions we have posed are deliberately not too searching but are to be used as starting points to establish a voyage of discovery and so allow you to accept criticism and observation with a more positive outlook.

Always remember that there are no absolute wrongs and rights in the world of performance – all work is subjective.

SPEAKING VOICE

How would you describe your own speaking voice?

| |
| |

Identify any of the following or add your own comments, if appropriate:

Rate of speech	fast	slow	just right
Articulation	excellent	just right	poor
Dynamics (volume)	too loud	too soft	just right
Pitch	too high	too low	varied
Inflection/pitch variety	monotone	sing-song	just right
Overall voice quality	excellent	moderate	poor

Identify any comments that have been made about your speaking voice during your voice classes.

1	
2	
3	
4	
5	

Do you feel any of the following descriptive phrases might apply to your own speaking voice? If your vocal quality is not mentioned below, place a description of your voice in the appropriate space:

breathy/sexy tone	very resonant	gasps for air
pleasant sound	grating sound	heavy accent
clears throat regularly	growling sound	throaty
musical quality	nasal quality	raspy quality

SINGING VOICE

How would you describe your own singing voice?

Identify any of the following or add your own comments, if appropriate:

Breathing	feels too high in the chest	feels too low in the chest	varied
Articulation	excellent	just right	poor
Dynamics (volume)	too loud	too soft	just right

Pitch	strain for high notes	squeeze for low notes	
Inflection/pitch variety	monotone	sing-song	just right
Overall voice quality	excellent	moderate	poor
Posture	rigid	collapsed	just right

Identify any comments that have been made about your singing voice during your singing classes.

1	
2	
3	
4	
5	

Do you feel any of the following descriptive phrases might apply to your own speaking voice? If your vocal quality is not mentioned below, place a description of your voice in the appropriate space:

breathy tone	very resonant	gasps for air
pleasant sound	grating sound	heavy accent
clears throat regularly	nasal quality	raspy quality

MOVEMENT

How would you describe your own movement? Do your physical gestures communicate any skills or activities, e.g. playing a musical instrument, fitness, weightlifting, running, dancing, etc.

Identify any of the following or add your own comments, if appropriate:

Rate of body movement	fast	slow	just right	
Gestures	head	body	arms	
Eye contact	direct	indirect	comfortable	
Physical centre	pelvis	upper body	head	
Standing posture – weight on	right leg	left leg	both legs	
Overall physical quality	jerky	fluid	Just right	

Identify any comments that have been made about your movement during class.

1	
2	
3	
4	
5	

Do you feel any of the following descriptive phrases might apply to your own movement? If a movement quality is not mentioned below, place a description of your movement in the appropriate space:

demonstrates with hands	quick movements	slow movements
walks fast	walks slowly	active facial expression
expressive body	easy to imitate	difficult to imitate
heavy movement	light movement	inactive facial expression

These questions and activities should have made you aware of what you bring physically to the process of being a student of Musical Theatre and of what you may need to develop. There is nothing to be ashamed of if you feel that you lack certain qualities and nothing boastful about being aware of your abilities. All aspects of your 'self' are of value and deserve to be nurtured.

The self and the song: Compiling and developing your portfolio

From the outset of your studies, it is important for you to identify a wide variety of songs that are suited to your voice and abilities so that you have an ever-increasing resource of performance material. By the time you have worked your way through the contents of this book, it is hoped that you will have compiled a substantial collection of pieces of Musical Theatre taken from all the major forms and periods that we shall describe. These will enable you to be prepared for auditions and performance opportunities of many kinds and will ensure that you can demonstrate a wide range of skills.

As an initial exercise respond to the following tasks:

- Name a song you know well that comes from a musical.
- What is the full name of the work/show?
- Who wrote the words of the song?
- Who wrote the dialogue for the musical?
- Who composed the music?
- When was the work/show written?
- Where and when is the action set?

Having completed this exercise you will realise that there is a wealth of information to be gleaned from just one lyric. So you can begin to imagine the complex and fascinating journey to be had as you unravel the elements of the entire musical.

We strongly suggest that you include in your portfolio some suitable examples from all the types of song and musical we describe in Chapter 5, 'The Anatomy of the Musical'.

Caring for the 'Self'

Before we move on to think about some more complex and abstract aspects of 'self', we need to consider ways in which we can care for our bodies and voices as they confront the challenges of your chosen profession. Your body and your voice are expressive, unique and very valuable instruments without which no performance is possible, and you have a responsibility to care for them and increase their potential. Even though your teachers may make suggestions for suitable exercises, it is only **you** who can create the time and space to do them on a regular basis, so that they become an integral part of your life and work.

Now think about three key aspects of caring for your physical self: lifestyle, relaxation and warm-up routines; as you approach your studies at a high level, you need to give honest answers to some searching questions about these aspects of your life.

Lifestyle

The last thing we are going to suggest is that, in order to become a successful performer, you must adopt a dreary and joyless lifestyle. However, the choices you make about how you live from day to day may profoundly affect your level of achievement. The most important factor is your level of personal organisation, particularly as it affects your use of time and space. How, when and where do you study or practice? How do you organise your personal space so that you do not waste time losing things? Do you give yourself time for nutritious meals or simply grab some 'fast food' on the run? Do you get adequate sleep or are you always too tired to concentrate or master a difficult song? Are you punctual and how do you organise your travel? Do you always keep others waiting? Do you live a balanced life? Are there built-in periods of quiet and reflection in your life or is it always hectic and noisy?

You can see from these questions (and there are more to come!) that although your 'private' life is really your business, the way in which you choose to live has enormous implications for your work as a student.

So take some time to think about the following:

How would you describe your own lifestyle?

Identify any of the following or add your own comments, if appropriate:

Sleep patterns	deep	shallow	erratic	number of hours
Fluids	ice-cold water	fizzy drinks	milk	alcohol
Diet	chocolate	vegetables	fresh fruit	cheese
Health signals	coughing	sinus	blocked nose	laryngitis
Mood	calm	tense	erratic	excited

Identify any comments that you have considered about your lifestyle and how it has impacted upon your performance ability.

1	
2	
3	
4	
5	

Do you feel any of the following descriptive phrases might apply to your own lifestyle? Do you agree or disagree? You might like to add to the list some more phrases that might apply to you personally. How are you going to reflect upon these in order to develop a personal understanding of the importance of your lifestyle?

It's fine to smoke	It's ok to drink before singing	I use throat lozenges
I steam twice a day	I need to be patient/calm	Whispering is bad for the voice
My low range is weak	I cough a lot	I suffer heartburn/hay fever
I am not sure about my weight	Avoid rooms with air conditioning	I go to the gym on a regular basis

Relaxation

We all know that movement emerges out of stillness and sound from silence but how do you, as a performer, ensure that you have that calm centre of relaxation on which to build? Many pressures in our daily lives bring tensions to our bodies and especially to our voices and these can so easily become 'locked in' and hinder or even damage our ability to perform. Techniques for release and relaxation are an essential part of your development in Musical Theatre: they will enable you to focus your energy, increase your vocal power and deepen your characterisation. They will ensure that you are always achieving your maximum potential in physical, emotional and vocal aspects of a performance. You will almost certainly encounter a variety of suggested approaches to relaxation: they may well be based on ancient oriental techniques such as yoga and t'ai chi or on the more recent Alexander technique, Feldenkrais or Pilates. You may first encounter these in a dance class or a sung/spoken voice class, and, invariably, there will be an emphasis on deep and efficient breathing. It is no coincidence that breathing in is described as 'Inspiration' because without it we simply cannot function.

However you first acquire knowledge, and understanding of relaxation is less important than how you absorb it into your life as a vital part of your self.

The following questions will help to establish where you have reached in that part of your journey:

Express your own ideas about relaxation? What are the essential differences between your own physical and mental well-being in both performance and everyday activities, e.g. use of breath, tension and release?

Identify any of the following or add your own comments, if appropriate:

Breathing patterns	fast	slow	erratic	just right
Where do you feel tension?	neck	shoulders	legs	hands
Emotional state – happy	relaxed	tense	passive	just right
Emotional state – sad	relaxed	tense	passive	just right
Breath intake	nose	mouth	low breath	high breath
Postural habits	spine	shoulders	lower body	neck

Identify any advice given to you concerning your physical and mental state of relaxation.

1
2
3
4
5

Do you feel any of the following phrases might apply to you when considering your body and the importance of relaxation to your own performance work? Do you agree or disagree? You might like to add to the list some more phrases that might apply to you personally. How are you going to reflect upon these in order to develop a personal understanding of the importance of relaxation?

butterflies in your stomach	tension in neck and shoulders	legs shake when seated
worried and anxious	physical fitness	regular practice
good breathing rhythm	take your time	are you often sick?

(continued)

importance of sleep	focus on what you are doing	keep thoughts positive

Warm-ups

If you are taking your training seriously, you will have discovered how physically and mentally demanding the world you have chosen to enter can be. We have already likened you to an athlete, and, in common with all athletes, it is vital in support of your training that you regularly warm up before attempting to perform at peak level.

As with relaxation, you will probably have gone through a number of warm-up routines with your various teachers, but you need to transform their advice into a habit that is as natural to you as breathing. In order to do this, you will need to plan your time so that the essential warm-up process is not overlooked and take personal responsibility for your own practice. The idea that you would not warm up properly before any kind of performance or intensive practical work should be totally foreign to your whole approach. But what is the best system for you to adopt?

The period of warm-up should act as a frontier and transition between your normal, everyday activities and your professional performance work. You may have been reading, writing or engaged in very static tasks for a long period or had a difficult journey to the theatre. You may not have used your voice in a large room or engaged in any physical activity for some time. You may have forgotten to breathe deeply or have been in a tense situation. All that must be left behind as you prepare for your performance: your personal instrument must now be tuned and all your energies gathered to focus on the task ahead.

We shall be providing a system for vocal warm-ups in Chapter 3.

To help you to think about and prepare for this process consider these questions:

How would you describe your own warm-up regime? Identify ten progressive exercises completed in any of your sessions, e.g. movement, voice (sung/spoken), acting. Suggest why these are now important to you and to your warm-up regime. Discuss their overall benefit to the body and voice of the performer.

Identify any of the following or add your own comments, if appropriate:

Important areas to develop in a warm-up regime				
Breath	intake	capacity	support	

Vocal onset	simultaneous	glottal	aspirate	
Articulation – vowels/consonants	tongue	teeth	lips	
Posture	relaxed	balanced	tension	

Identify any comments that have been made about your warm-up regime before taking class.

1	
2	
3	
4	
5	

Do you feel any of the following phrases might apply to your own warm-up regime? Do you agree or disagree? You might like to add to the list some more phrases that might apply to you personally. How are you going to reflect upon these in order to develop a personal understanding of the importance of the warm-up?

important to sing scales	tension in body	clear articulation
vocally free	resonant tone	too much breath
too little breath	vocal agility	know your vocal limits
not enough sleep	good posture	breath support

Self and the inner life

Everyone who is reading this book is a unique human being and nobody else can bring to the challenge of Musical Theatre precisely the same qualities and experiences that you can. It is worth reminding yourself of your unique value every day: you may have been made aware of this sense through a religious faith or through the findings of science or even by reading these words, but however you have arrived at this recognition, it is an essential part of creating a concept of 'self'. We have seen that some aspects of self are largely physical – forming an expressive and subtle outward appearance and capability – but if you were to try to define what precisely makes your 'self', it would most probably involve what we might call your 'inner life'.

Interestingly, this is a concept often used by actors, and we also employ two terms with theatre origins to define aspects of the inner life: **character** (a person involved in a drama) and **personality** (taken from the Greek word for a theatrical mask). The definitions of these two words can be slippery, but most people would agree that our character consists of the innate qualities that make us what we are and that our personality describes the way in which we relate to the world around us. As an actor, you will frequently be expected to explore and inhabit the inner life of a character and to demonstrate that character's personality in your performance, so it is important to understand the influences that shape our inner lives. This is certainly not a textbook of psychology but we can draw valuable insights from developments in this field and from the related field of psychotherapy.

The two factors which will have shaped and will continue to shape your inner life are your **genetic/physical make-up**, some of which may be inherited, and your **experiences** from the time of your birth. Long before the discovery of DNA or the development of psychology, thinkers recognised that the very early years of life and particularly our relationship with parents helped to shape human character, and this led to the debate concerning **nature** and **nurture**. We still use aspects of these sometimes conflicting concepts when we say 'Oh, it's just in my nature' on the one hand, or 'Well, it's just how I was brought up' on the other. The important factor for you as a student/actor is to understand that there are some things that you cannot change but that by careful reflection you can modify their impact on your behaviour by recognising how they have shaped your attitudes and approaches.

In order to think creatively about your inner life and that of any character you are aiming to portray, it may be helpful to draw upon the work of the famous psychoanalyst Carl Jung, who was particularly interested in character types and in those unseen and often unconscious inner drives that determine how we behave. He divided aspects of the creation of 'self' into *Eigenwelt*, *Mitwelt* and *Umwelt*. We suggest that you take each of these and apply it to your self for a moment.

Eigenwelt is what we would recognise as our essential 'self'. It is how you see yourself and is constituted from your genetics and biological make-up (your 'nature') and from your experiences (your 'nurture'). The *Eigenwelt* will be determined by how you treat your body, your diet, how and what you learn and by everything you say, do and think. Your *Eigenwelt* is totally unique even if you are an identical twin or have had some common experiences with others.

In the box below, describe as many of the aspects of your *Eigenwelt* as possible.

```



```

What aspects of the *Eigenwelt* can you NOT describe?

```



```

Mitwelt (**sometimes called** *Mittelwel*) is your immediate environment: it is where you are reading this book, the sounds you can hear, the things you can smell, feel or touch. It is the temperature of your surroundings and the effect your environment has on your mood or actions. It is how you respond to everything and everybody around you in order to survive and the thought processes you go through in order to make decisions, the feelings and dreams you experience and the patterns of sleep and concentration you adopt because of what is close to you. As a student of Musical Theatre, you will have a very active relationship between your *Eigenwelt* and *Mitwelt*.

In the box below, record every aspect of your current *Mitwelt* that you think is affecting you at this moment.

How does the environment shape your behaviour, and is your current *Mitwelt* appropriate for what you are trying to achieve?

Umwelt is the wider universe of which you are a part. It is made known to you through news bulletins, exploration, cameras and belief systems. You may try to make sense of it through myths and beliefs. It may well be an aspect of your upbringing and culture, and its influences will often be powerful and difficult to recognise at first. It is your concept of yourself as part of the human race and it will determine your attitudes to world events. Your *Eigenwelt* responds to the news and information that emanate from the *Umwelt*: they are the universal backdrop to your personal life.

In the box below, describe how you see your 'self' as part of a wider universe.

What feelings does being part of something so vast provoke in your *Eigenwelt*?

Language, thought and action

All of this may seem a very long way from studying Musical Theatre but think for a moment of one of the most famous moments in a stage musical, the opening song of *Oklahoma!* (1943) with words by Oscar Hammerstein II and music by Richard Rogers. Against the trend of many musicals of the period, this begins not with a chorus but with a solo. The stage directions tell us: *Stage left, an old woman churning butter. Off-stage right, the voice of a lone cowboy singing 'Oh What a Beautiful Morning'.*

In that song, Curly, the cowboy, describes his *Mitwelt*. It is a beautiful day, there is a 'bright, golden haze on the meadow' and the 'corn is as high as an elephant's eye'. But the effect on his *Eigenwelt* is profound: the sights and sounds make him convinced that 'everything's going my way' and that his place in the wide universe is one of peace and happiness. His positive position in the *Umwelt* creates a huge sense of well-being.

If you are required to sing this song, **every one** of these factors must be taken into consideration whether or not you chose to use the precise terms we have employed.

On the surface, this opening song of *Oklahoma!* may seem lacking in action. The cowboy does, in fact, enter during his song and we see him standing on or moving a little around the stage. But you need to understand that words **are** actions and that all words and actions are the product of **thought**. Even though a character is not moving or dancing, if they are speaking or singing, they are engaged in a form of action that must have been initiated by a thought process. This forms part of a character's **motivation**. Thinking is just as much an **action** as a **gesture**.

Performance psychologists, such as those employed by Olympic teams, increasingly understand that what we are thinking profoundly affects how we are feeling and those thoughts and feelings will find expression in action. In the case of an athlete, a positive feeling may well result in running faster or jumping higher, but in everyday life our thoughts and feeling mainly culminate in words. In Musical Theatre, the use of words will be heightened by their being highly selective and, in many cases, sung. So to return to our example, the positive thoughts inspired in Curly by the beautiful weather and the sounds and sights of nature create very good feelings and those result in some memorable and expressive words. Combined with a simple yet unforgettable melody, they combine to make one of the seminal moments of Musical Theatre.

We shall be exploring the nature and importance of both spoken and sung words in Chapters 4 and 5. ,

Here are some final questions to consider:

- How would you describe your 'personality'?
- Does this reflect your real 'character', or do you sometimes hold tension between your inner feelings and the outward show?
- What aspects of your character affect your work as a student? Are you, for instance: lazy; well organised; unable to take criticism; good at working with others; easily discouraged; able to focus and concentrate for long periods; able to learn words easily; confident; insecure; any other features?
- How well do you use words? Do you enjoy listening to skilled speakers? Do you have a 'regional accent', and, if so, does this affect how you feel about yourself?

2 *Understanding Performance*

3 The Beginning of the Process

Let us start from the very beginning of the day and see how we prepare for our work as a Musical Theatre student.

A really good acting exercise is to remember exactly every minute detail of getting up in the morning and preparing to leave home for college. This exercise can be thought of in many ways and there are several reasons to justify it – let us just take the simplest one for the time being – the personal preparation from the beginning of the day for the early singing tutorial at 9:00 a.m.

Usually, we prepare for the day by having a shower, dressing and possibly (of course) checking what we look like in the mirror. But there are other additional factors such as the tensions of the day, the realisation that perhaps we are going to be late, have not prepared for the singing session, can't find the music for the song or have forgotten to write up a session for the acting class later the same day. No matter what happens in your own personal preparation for the day, finally you leave home and go to college. It is, in fact, very revealing for you to map out your own personal activities and the spirit in which you leave home to go to class.

An initial exercise

Remember and write down exactly everything you do from the time you get out of bed to leaving home. Create a short scene by acting out these events in the space of your own bedroom. (Your stage set is already designed.) This is a very beneficial acting exercise because it enables you to use your own experiences and challenge the detail and accuracy of the actions and intentions within your own scene. If you are going to present this work, it is essential that you play this scene over and over again until it is absolutely perfect in every detail. Then you can even play it out to an audience in a neutral space, recreating the environment in which you are familiar.

What can we learn from this?

You travel to college and embark upon your working day with a set of mental images, tensions and worries. You may finally arrive for your singing tutorial just on time. What comes next is perhaps the most important aspect of the class – 'the warm-up'. It is important to remember that this will not always be the responsibility of your teacher. It is vital that you prepare yourself for the singing tutorial in the most positive and effective manner, and this will enable you to make the most of the allocated time with your teacher.

It is probable that the first few singing sessions will be spent working out a useful daily regime that you will eventually be able to complete on your own prior to any singing lesson. If you follow this regime, you will eventually be allowing more time for the detailed work of developing vocal technique and your artistry.

Why worry about posture?

If you recognise anything of the situation we described, you will have arrived at the singing lesson dressed as 'you' with all your tensions and physical habitual gestures – possibly caused by the heavy bag on your shoulder, books carried from the library or that late-night computer game. As you look in the mirror, you will recognise the same person who left your home only hours earlier. Nothing has changed – you are still you! Look at your shoulders – one might be lower than the other – why? The heavy bag might be the source of this misery. Now the magic of **alignment** has to happen. You are required to balance the efforts between various muscles in order to transform both your physical and vocal being into a creative and inspirational vehicle for artistic communication – you are to become a singer. How is this going to be achieved?

Posture is one of the most important factors to be considered in preparing the body and the vocal mechanism for the work of the day (Figures 3.1 and 3.2). Stand in front of a mirror and now be much more aware of your physical shape when standing in order to allow breath to enter your body in a relaxed and calm manner. Check for signs of tension in your neck and shoulders and be aware of any lifting of the upper chest when breathing in that might also impact upon shoulder tension. However, do be aware that posture is not just about standing straight and being upright; it is a question of being flexible and allowing the human body to have a natural set of balanced relationships in a fluid state.

Figure 3.1: *Leaving the bedroom dressed, bag on shoulder*

Figure 3.2: *Entering the singing studio, bag on shoulder*

Exercise 1

Look at how you stand when getting ready to sing (Figures 3.3–3.7 show different poses).

Did you notice any of these signs: (i) feet too far apart and toes clutching at the floor, (ii) knees locked, (iii) feet too close together lacking in balance and insecure in posture and (iv) weight shifting from left side of body to right side. If you did notice any of these in your own physical posture, aim to correct them by reflecting the appropriate features of the figures below.

You must be aware that this is vitally important for your creative and artistic work even though it may appear to have little purpose at the beginning of your journey. As your workload increases, this neutral state will become more and more important to your performance.

Figure 3.3: *Good posture with feet apart and matching shoulders*

Figure 3.4: *Legs too wide*

Figure 3.5: *Knees locked and tight*

Figure 3.6: *Standing with too much tension throughout the body, could fall over if pushed*

Figure 3.7: *Too relaxed and casual with weight on one leg*

To understand how tension really works, try these simple exercises and monitor how they feel in your body.

Exercise 2

Question: Have you ever wondered why we are sometimes immediately not able to answer a simple question to which we have recently heard the answer? Why do we remember it ten minutes later?

Answer: We may not trust ourselves. We have too much self-doubt, and as a result this transfers into general physical and emotional tension.

- Find an article from a book or journal that you have been reading lately. Read a few sentences out loud before beginning the exercise. Try to remember the patterns created as you speak.
- With your index finger on both your right and left hand, tap alternate fingers in an even measure 1–2–3–4–5–6–7–8 and then use your right and left finger to create the same pattern RLRLRLRL evenly on a table top. Keep this rhythm going for as long as you can.
- Now read the passage again in a natural spoken delivery. Try to get to the end of the passage.

Did you succeed?

Did an inner voice get you to try harder? Did you start to ignore the rhythm? Was one finger hitting the table with more weight? Did your speaking voice try and imitate the rhythmic pattern?

- Do it again and don't criticise yourself too harshly – just relax and aim to read the passage in a natural way and keep the internal rhythm going at the same time.

Did you succeed?

Were you aware of uneven pressure and tension between the right and left hand?

- Do it again but this time whenever you find yourself trying too hard to either speak naturally or get the rhythm correct, don't stop but focus your awareness on a single element of the exercise at one time. Concentrate on speaking naturally or concentrate on the rhythmic pulse. Observe your body and try to release the tensions being created by the conflicting tasks and relax.

Exercise 3

Hold out your arm and turn the palm of your right hand to an upright position. Gradually curl the fingers into the centre of your palm with your thumb covering your fingertips until your hand is shaking with tension. (Do this to the count of 10.) At this moment, slightly decrease the tension in your grip. (Count 10–9.) You will almost certainly feel a sense of 'release'. However, are you to believe that there is now no tension in the rest of the grip? No, in fact until the hand is returned to the opening position, the tension is not completely released. (Release the grip to the count of 8–1 to demonstrate this.)

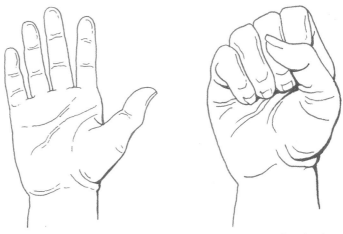

Figure 3.8: *Open palm*   **Figure 3.9:** *Closed palm*

This is a perfect example of how much unnecessary tension we hold in our bodies and how important it is to achieve a complete release of unwanted tension before the performance work can be completed efficiently (Figures 3.8 and 3.9).

Use your time as a student wisely so that the later part of your career is safe and secure in all aspects. You do not want to be like many talent show success stories and pop stars who can sing well for six weeks, and then have to be replaced because they have not had adequate vocal and physical training to prepare them for the daily regime of a working actor-singer. You surely want to be the artiste who can sing for six years and hopefully for sixty years. Your destiny is in your own hands – quite literally!

General comment

Because we have suggested that your destiny is in your own hands, we should consider the importance and relevance of our hands in all our performance and presentation work. Hands are crucial to a relaxed, honest, truthful and balanced performance. They are inextricably linked with the arms and hence the shoulders and so our hands clearly contribute to and signal to the observer a balanced and natural posture. If you are unsure of what to do with your hands, then you are probably in need of rethinking your entire upper body posture. Your mental preparation for the work undertaken, whether singing or speaking, needs further clarification and purpose. The tendency is to push yourself physically towards the audience in order to identify your thoughts and personality. Yet, by doing this, you are physically disturbing the natural suspension between the muscles within your body. Always think about making the audience 'come to you', in order that you can carry them forward in the line of action and truth being expressed. A perfect spatial balance between audience and performer is as important as a perfect balance within the body of the performer.

Neutral posture and breath

Before beginning any of these exercises stand in a natural relaxed stance. Let your breath enter your body calmly and then allow the air to flow out of your body. Do this several times until you have a feeling of calm in your physical being often too much. Too much is spoken *about* breathing, but it is essential that you understand how and why you breathe before making extra demands upon your body for the purpose of singing. We manage quite well in our everyday world, so why not also in our singing world? Clearly there are demands to be made in singing that will not be required in our everyday existence but still, we must not create stressful situations simply in order to sing! What we must take care **not to do**, is to over-exert our breathing mechanism so that undue tension is brought upon the larynx, forcing it upwards within the throat. This process may produce some useful short-term developments such as a wider upper range but the voice will soon probably lose its colour and become harsh, finally suffering from sub-glottal pressure.

In order to enable this essential breath to take place, it sometimes helps to think of the delicate sweet-smelling perfume of a rose, or something that attracts you, so that you enjoy the physical and sensual art of breathing in through your nose. In effect the intake of breath becomes the inspirational thought on which all your work is soon to be based. Eventually, the value and uniqueness of your thought is what will make your work original and attractive to the ear of your audiences. However, always remember that you don't need to take a breath to prepare for a dramatic moment in your life. What often happens is that the dramatic event takes place and then the body recovers (requiring a greater intake of breath) in order to enable life to continue.

If you do not prepare your body and breathing appropriately, your response to the music and words being sung or spoken could tend towards over-breathing. By taking in too much oxygen, you then cause an imbalance with the required amount of carbon dioxide in your body and so your entire personal chemical balance is disturbed.

You need to be relaxed and calm but still be active and alert physically and mentally. Your chest needs to be lifted and the breath needs to feel as if going low in your body.

It is important that your body is trained to understand the cause and effect of any event that is likely to happen to it. It is in the rehearsal and training that the body is prepared for each breathing event, and when things go wrong (such as singing flat or poor phrasing) it is the correction of these faults that will enable the breathing process to work more effectively. The connection between mind and body are crucial in this work, and the preparation and understanding of both text and music are integral to the overall technique of the actor-singer.

Exercise 4

Lift your arms above your head and let your fingers spread with energy like a puppet being pulled by its strings trying to touch the ceiling. Look up to the ceiling and let your heels lift off the ground and stand on your toes as if being pulled up to the sky by your fingertips. Give yourself a moment and then imagine that someone has cut the strings and so your arms drop down by the side of your body. (Be sure to let your hands fall naturally to your side.) Keep the rest of the body in exactly the same position, and feet also. Now, keeping the eyes looking upwards, lower the heels so that they rest on the floor and you have an equal balance between toe and heel. Now lower the head gently until the eyes are in a natural position – avoid a double chin (i.e. too low). Now you are physically prepared and excited to sing.

Now that you have completed these exercises, give yourself a body shake in order to remove any small pockets of tension in your body. Walk around the room and come back to the mirror – you will notice a difference in your posture and alignment and possibly be amazed by your height!

Exercise 5

Having established the importance of balance, posture and breath, some exercises to help you develop and strengthen these techniques will assist you in your discovery of the voice. It is good to remember that there is always a danger, when starting to sing, that you release too much breath too soon and so have insufficient control to get to the end of a phrase. Surprisingly, this rarely happens when you speak – when have you ever been out of breath when shouting at a friend or trying to establish yourself in an important argument? You seem to be able to go on and on until you have finished your line of thought. However, when you sing, it appears to be a completely different matter. The following exercises will help you develop a breathing technique that will support you when you are required to sing a complete thought or phrase.

5(a) As you make this regular hissing 'ss' sound, you should note that there are no vibrations at all in your throat. This sound is known as 'unvoiced':

5(b) Now try the same exercise with a short humming sound 'mm':

What do you notice in your throat as you make this humming sound? You will notice vibrations in your throat. This sound is known as 'voiced'.

Before trying out the next musical exercise speak out loud both 'p' and 'b'. Notice that your lips are in the same position for both sounds but they will feel different. This is because 'p' is an unvoiced sound, with no vibration as in 'ss'; and 'b' is a voiced sound, like the 'mm' exercise. Try this exercise:

5(c) Now try this exercise:

p   b   p   b   p b p   b p b   m   b   m   p   p   b   p b m

5(d) Now try this exercise mixing up all the voiced and unvoiced sounds:

p   b   p b p   ss   ss   p   b p   b ss   ss   p   b   ss ss m

5(e) Now add an 'ah' sound to every consonant and aim for a smoother, slower legato style of singing. Work out when to breathe!

pah   bah   pah   bah   pah   ssah   bah

pah   bah   pah   bah   ssah   ssah   pah   bah   ssah   ssah   mah

5(f) Now add 'm' to every 'ah' sound in order to establish what is known as 'forward placement'. This is generally required when the singer needs to make the sound bright and energetic and is most relevant to the 'musical theatre sound'.

mah   mah   mah   mah   mah   mah   mah

mah   mah   mah   mah   mah   mah   mah   mah   mah   mah   mah

5(g) Why not create your own vocal exercises using phrases from songs you know well to explore the voiced and unvoiced sounds?

N.B. *Remember to stand with your feet apart and your knees soft rather than locked (as demonstrated in Figure 3.3 or 3.4) Sing the same melody again. Try to think about the quality of the intake of breath and a sense of warmth in your voice.*

Exercise 6

(a) Now that you are aware of the need for a correct posture, consider any short phrase from a song you know well and, using the sound 'ah', sing the melody unaccompanied looking at yourself in the mirror. What did you notice about your physical presence and delivery? Now sing the same phrase to 'Yah', 'Bah' and 'Yum'. Look in the mirror and watch the shape of your mouth. Try to let the 'Yah' sound create a more relaxed jaw so that your mouth drops down in a north to south position rather than spread like a smile across your face – east to west. Be happy but sound warm . . .

Did you notice any difference between the two versions? If so, what? Perhaps your standing position was slightly different. Your facial expression might have been tenser in the first version. Did you feel tightness in the jaw or tension over the eyes? Where were your hands? These are all areas that might require attention. However, take it slowly; you cannot expect to achieve a perfect vocal technique within a few weeks! Physical 'flaws' cannot and should not change immediately – be gentle and work hard to overcome each technical point in turn. Aim to keep an element of surprise in your vocal work and always be alert in your thoughts. This will make all the difference to your natural sound.

- Sing each phrase again this time using the words of the lyric, trying to keep your body calm from obvious tension and yet excited in order to bring the performance to life. Did that feel better?

Too much to take in? Overall, yes, there is: but these skills and knowledge can only be absorbed over a period of time. Use the first year of your studies to be completely aware of these basic pointers and the rest will fall into place as you progress.

CHECKLIST BEFORE SINGING

- ☐ Raise, then lower arms upwards and out to restore high chest position needed for singing.
- ☐ Stretch arms overhead, then bend down and stretch towards the floor. Slowly rise up one vertebra at a time until standing posture – high chest.
- ☐ Rotate shoulders from left to right. Then both shoulders. Raise your head so that it is in line with your spinal column, and not tilted up or down.
- ☐ Stand with feet apart. *(Is your weight evenly balanced?)*
- ☐ Knees unlocked. *(Can you bend them easily?)*
- ☐ Back straight. *(Are you standing erect, comfortably and not stiffly?)*
- ☐ Head erect. *(Is your chin level, not too far up or down?)*
- ☐ Ribcage lifted. *(Is your chest high and able to expand?)*
- ☐ Shoulders relaxed. *(Are they comfortably down, not too far forward or back?)*
- ☐ Hands at your side. *(Are they relaxed and free of tension?)*
- ☐ Feel you are being pulled up by a string in the crown of your head – lengthen the neck, etc.

Having checked these points and established a regime for gaining a neutral position, it is time to consider some basic breathing techniques that will support you throughout your first few months of training.

When the body is balanced and in a neutral position, the vocal work will become easier and have an exciting energy. You will also have more power and be able to sing longer vocal phrases with ease. You should be aware that appropriate footwear is sometimes an important factor in the success of the developing singer: shoes with high heels should be avoided and this includes boots for the men. There is often a danger of tipping the body forwards so that the toes tend to try to grip the floor in order to retain a good balance. You must remove all this unnecessary tension.

Exercise 7

Although we all know that we are constantly required to move in musical theatre for these exercises stand in front of the mirror and observe any physical reactions to the following actions:

First Action: Breathe in through your nose and exhale slowly on a soft humming 'voiced' sound or 8 slow counts. What did you notice?

You will have noticed that the upper part of your chest lifted – this is known as **clavicular** *breathing.*

Second Action: Breathe in through your mouth and exhale slowly on a soft humming sound for 8 slow counts. What did you notice?

You will have noticed that the breath went lower in the body and the shoulders were not so active. This is known as **diaphragmatic** *breathing and should be encouraged at all times.*

Third Action: Breathe gently in through your nose on the count of 3, and then on the final count of 4 breathe through the mouth, and exhale slowly on a soft humming sound for 8 slow counts. What did you notice?

This combining of both styles of breathing allows for a full response and avoids cold breath on the vocal folds. It also looks better on the stage and concert platform. There is nothing worse than looking like an excited foreigner trying to give directions to a lost traveller or a floundering fish gasping for air.

There are many other points to consider here but taking breath in through the mouth has the potential to dry out the vocal folds: we should aim for a combination of both nose and mouth breathing appropriate to the work being sung and to keep the body 'topped up' for the performance. The most important point to remember when breathing in to sing, is to draw as much attention away from the throat as possible.

We need to activate the Third Action (see above) with a more relaxed style of breathing in order to get our breath as low in the body as possible and yet not interfere with our facial expressions. These are to be required for the emotional journey of the character and song at a later point in our learning.

Figure 3.10 shows correct posture and support Figure 3.11 shows incorrect posture and support.

Further exercises

Breathe in through the nose for the even count of 1–2–3 and on the 4th beat breathe through the mouth. Exhale gently. Repeat this exercise several times.

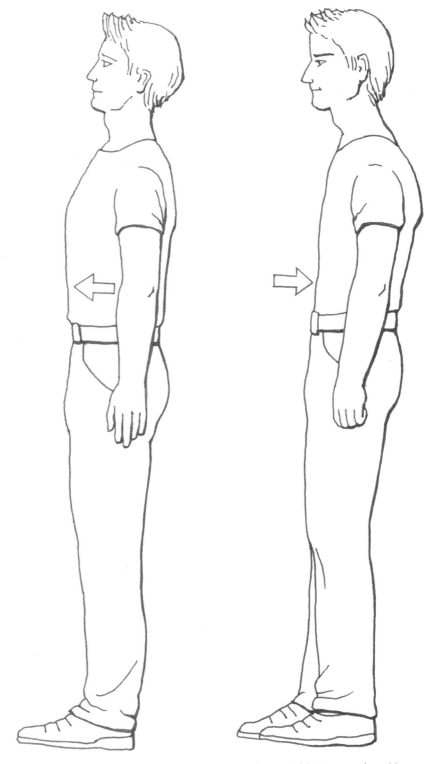

Figure 3.10: *Correct breathing*   **Figure 3.11:** *Incorrect breathing*

Now repeat the same in breath routine 1–2–3 (nose) and 4 (mouth) and exhale on 8 beats.

sh	sh	sh	sh	shee	
sh	sh	sh	sh	shaa	
sh	sh	sh	sh	shoo	

Points to consider

- Listen for a steady and even sound
- No movement in shoulders
- Abdomen should expand

Finally yawn silently and then audibly a few times to conclude this section of work to open throat and relax.

Note of warning

We are reluctant to mention the 'yawn' because although it actions the required muscles in the mouth, it often indicates a tired thought process and has the opposite effect on the singer to the one required. However, if you can consider an excited breath with anticipation then all will be well.

Exercise 8

A good technical exercise to develop a useful level of breathing together with resonance is as follows. (This requires you to first consider breathing through the nose and calming down the lifting chest movement that is so akin to this method of breathing.)

Place one hand on your upper chest and the other on your abdomen and monitor when the breath is high. Every time the breath lifts your upper chest, continue with the exercise, but as you continue, try to get the breath lower in the body and to release any lift in the upper chest. There will be times when you feel great tension and at other times this will be released. Just keep going until you are totally calm and released with the low breath.

A very important point to remember at this stage

If you are working on your own and the problem persists after several attempts, stop, rest, change exercise and come back to it fresh later. This way you will help to avoid continually reinforcing the error. Make a note, and bring it up at your next lesson. Persevere: it is in the doing that you conquer the technique. If you keep stopping and starting, the body becomes the victor, and so it takes you longer to overcome the point of technique being tackled. This applies to all singing work whether in training or in actual performance. Always keep going! Sometimes it is essential to listen to your teacher whilst singing in order that the fault can be effectively discussed. Stop singing and the sound and the problem have also stopped.

A further valuable exercise

Alternate a sniff though the nose with an out breath through the mouth and lips on the sounds of 'm' [<u>M</u>UM],'n' [<u>N</u>UN], 'ny' [E<u>NY</u>A] and 'ng' [SI<u>NG</u>]. Note the position of the tongue with the teeth as you sing these four nasal continuants. Try to work out where the tongue is placed in the mouth so that you begin to combine both the physical and artistic in your performance work.

We hope that you discovered that the tongue moved from the front of the mouth to the back and then vice versa. The position of the tongue is always very important, and so this is a good exercise not only for breathing but also for tongue placement and resonance.

M tongue placed gently behind the lower teeth

N tongue lifted and placed behind the upper teeth

NY blade of tongue pushed against the hard palate

NG back of tongue spreads across the soft palate and so blocks the sound coming forwards

Advice: This is a good time to talk to your singing teacher about your progress.

The actual warm-up

You will discover in the next few pages some helpful exercises to create a technical and secure warm-up regime. These will certainly support you for the first year of your studies and enable you to get more benefit from your lessons.

You will discover that the best types of warm-up vocal exercises are a selection of those that allow the voice to execute:

- easy movement from one note to the next (slides),
- lip and tongue trills,
- scales with a variety of chosen open and closed vowel sounds such as:
  ee [as in b**EE**n] – eh [as in **E**ffort] – ah [as in sp**A**] – aw [as in s**AW**] – oo [as in b**OO**t]
  and
- staccato exercises based on arpeggio figures.
  'ee' [i], 'eh' [ɛ], 'ah' [a], 'aw' [ɔ] and 'oo' [u] are a mixture of tongue and lip vowels.
  'ee' [i] and 'oo' [u] are closed vowels; 'eh' [ɛ],'ah' [a] and 'aw' [ɔ] are open vowels.

Use your time wisely. So often we hear students practising scales, and when we ask them why they are singing in a specific way, they are unable to provide a clear answer. Singing exercises for thirty minutes of each day can be an utter waste of time unless you interrogate the reasons and the purpose behind them and actually use them effectively to develop the techniques in a scientific and secure manner. Make the most use of your time and try to understand why you are required to do the given exercises.

A point of interest

Exercise: Sing a scale on any vowel of your choosing.

Did you use the vowel 'AH'? Did you sing the scale ascending (going up)? If the answer is YES for either of these questions, you have surprisingly made life difficult for yourself.

Note that the 'AH' sound comes in the middle of the five vowels suggested above. That means that it has a specific placement within the mouth that needs to relate to preceding vowels and so may be not as easy as first thought. Be assured that EE would have been easier.

Did you sing your scale going upwards? **Yes!** Why make life difficult for yourself?

What is easier – climbing upstairs or coming downstairs? Think of Mary Poppins sliding down the banister. Why are there escalators in supermarkets going up but often we can only find stairs coming down? If it is harder in real life, why make singing also difficult? Always aim to sing warm-up exercises on **descending sliding scales**. In a warm-up exercise you are limbering up the vocal mechanism, not training it; so it is better to let the exercise be as easy and achievable as possible. Singing technique is where the actual vocal work has to be done and the detail of each exercise understood in detail.

However, it is important to realise that training to be a singer is as demanding as training to be an athlete, so little and often with regard to warm-ups and technique, is far more beneficial than the rushed practice session just before class. If you really cannot find the time to give at least 30–45 minutes a day to this preparatory work, then this is definitely not the career for you. In contrast, it is not wise to practise 2 hours a day for 7 seven days a week. You need to demonstrate good management of time in order to develop as an effective actor-singer.

Warm-up exercises

Note from the authors: *We have avoided giving too many specific written musical exercises as this rather disturbs the point of a warm-up regime suited to each individual. You will find your own examples and exercises to suit your voice as you progress through the early stages of your work. However, some melodic figures will be suggested owing to the demands of the exercise. You should actively research a regime of warm-up techniques and identify these in your own working practice schedule and discuss these with your teacher at several points throughout your studies to ensure they are effective for your needs.*

Warm-up 1: Gentle preparation for the vocal mechanism

1(a) Take a breath and just before you finish that intake of breath, begin to breathe out on an aspirate 'h'. This should be a sensation that you will always enjoy. It is as if you are constantly on the verge of something exciting. You will feel engaged with the act of both speaking and singing. The purpose of breath for performance is now a reality, and you are now breathing for performance rather than breathing to maintain life.

A word of warning: If you take a breath and then hold it before singing you will produce an incorrect balance with the glottis and the airflow and so the sound will sound quite aggressive and hard-edged. Sometimes you will hear a teacher say 'hold it!' mainly because that is what they want at that immediate moment and they are searching for words to communicate an immediate effect. Try and interpret that instruction as 'suspending the breath' rather than holding it and all will be well. This may well be a vocal quality to be used in the future; it is often used to demonstrate the sense of interaction between the singer and the thought process, e.g. 'I' as in 'I dreamed a dream' or 'If I loved you'. In both examples, the glottal accentuates the first person and so creates an emotional connection with the lyric. However, for the warm-up section, this tone is not welcome. *Be patient: it will all come together as soon as you are ready.* Also do not use songs as technical exercises because when you come to sing them in your own work you will find it difficult to reject the physical memory associated with a specific phrase.

Continue: Capture this gentle feeling of breathing in; then, before completion of the cycle, on an outgoing breath, form the sound of an 'h'. Do not think of any pitch. Now do this again, but this time after sounding the 'h' allow any pitched note that you can sing to be heard. Surprisingly, it will sound a little like 'huh' (the neutral vowel) rather than 'her' – always avoid the 'r' sound. Try to keep this note constant in tone and quality for the count of about 8 beats. You can extend the exercise by changing the vowel sounds as suggested previously – 'ee', 'eh', 'ah', 'oh' and 'oo'.

By repeating this very first exercise you are beginning to understand physically and emotionally the connection between the spoken and sung word, and so you are finding a natural place for your voice to work and communicate as an actor-singer. This is the point where the spoken voice transports itself into the sung world and so the truth of the text can still be communicated with skill and integrity. What you are in fact doing here is extending the primal sound of the human being and extending it into a vocal sound that can be elongated by pitch.

1(b) Using the same principle as above, breathe in and just before completion put teeth together and loosen the lips to create a hissing sound – remembering to place the 'h' before making the 's' sound [HSSSSSSSSSSSSSSSSSSS] on an outward breath.

This should give you a clear idea about how your body should feel when singing and will assist in developing your vocal work enormously.

Warm-up 2: The gentle slide

2(a) Allow the voice to sound a simple 'h' and neutral vowel sound, e.g. Huh.

Then extend this exercise by placing an 'h' in front of the 5 vowels already discussed above: 'ee', 'eh', 'ah', 'oh' and 'oo'.

(H)uh_____   H(ee)_____   H(ah)_____   H(ee)_____   H(ah)_____

Do not feel you have to sing these sounds; just let them happen naturally. Please remember that these are warm-up exercises. You need to explore the 'sigh' rather than the 'sung'.

2(b) Repeat these exercises with a falling 6th, 7th and octave leap.

(H)uh_____   H(ee)_____   H(ah)_____   H(ee)_____

What you need to feel when completing this warm-up exercise is the equality between the first and last note. If you find you are trying too hard at the bottom of the sigh, then you are not doing the exercise correctly, and you must return to smaller intervals until you have achieved this equality of pitch and tonal quality. This is vital for the future of your work.

This process is very important, and when you find you are not achieving the best results, you must return to the previous exercise and again start strengthening your vocal mechanism to adequately prepare you for your singing journey. This is why it is necessary to keep the warm-up regime exercise regular and at appropriate times during the day and week.

Warm-up 3: Lip buzz

Put the teeth together and think of creating a light buzzing sound and use the falling leap patterns as described in 2(b) to assist you in this work. Aim to create a very light 'S' sound which gradually develops into a 'zzzzzzzzzzz' sound. This should give you a good free feeling. Having mastered the slide, aim for a more specific note change as you descend as in exercise 3(a).

Szzz_____   Szzz_____   Szzz_____   Szzz_____

Now imagine you are feeling some cold wind and you are shaking yourself to warm yourself up. Another way is to clasp hands together in front of your chest and shake, causing a vibration when making an open 'ah' sound. Now put your lips together and make a 'brrrrrrrrrrr' sound. This is the beginning of the lip buzz and has the same effect on the vocal folds as the above exercise. However, now you must try to link notes together and negotiate gentle leaps as well in order to develop strength and to keep the sensation of a free and relaxed breath pressure placed firmly and securely at the front of your mouth – all sensation should be on your lips.

Warm-up 4: Tongue trill

Repeat the same exercises as for the lip buzz but now substitute the sound 'trrrrr' instead of 'brrrrr'.

Both exercises 3 and 4 encourage a loose jaw and a light controlled flow of air with no vocal tension at all. You must aim for this sensation before moving on. A few minutes spent mastering both the lip buzz and the tongue trill will enhance your future work enormously. Do not be worried if the tongue trill is perhaps a little more difficult. If you are having a problem with the tongue trill, it is essential that you consult your teacher to find alternative ways of tackling the exercise.

Remember that all these exercises must be done with as much care as possible.

Warm-up 5: Siren or slide

This is a popular vocal exercise and encourages the singer to open the vocal tract and to encourage a freedom of sound and pitch from the top to the bottom of the voice. Again remember that this is not a singing exercise. Take the nasal continuant NG and aim for a high note within your vocal range and descend slowly to the lowest notes in your range. Aim to develop this skill so that you are making contact with high and low notes with the same amount of pressure and intention. If you hear a slight creak in the voice, this is a moment to lift the pitch and return to the same place until you have smoothed out the little blemish in the scale. Many students when asked to siren open up the exercise onto an immediate vowel sound – do not attempt to do this! Always use the 'ng' sound for the warm-up exercise for the time being.

Warm-up 6: Humming

Think of the 'M' sound and the position of the tongue as explained above (Exercise 8). Try not to think of any specific vowel sound, and you will approximate the neutral vowel sound which is excellent for this type of work as it involves the least amount of movement to create. It is also known as the schwa sound (neutral) vowel but this can be explained later – it sounds like 'uh'.

If you want to double check you have got the vibration correct and a real sense of buzzing, put your finger on the lower lip and release from the upper lip. If the sound is the same then you have the perfect position for the exercise. You should also feel a buzz and a slight tickle in the nose, lips and face.

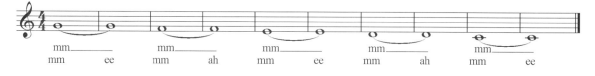

If you want to develop this exercise a little further to increase your awareness of resonance, try the other nasal continuants 'n', 'ny' and 'ng'. However, do not try to get louder using these extra exercises – aim to keep a constant tonal quality and resonant sensation.

Warm-up 7: *Messa di voce*

This is the same as the above exercise, but now you are required to get louder and softer to a specific number of counts. Remember the sighing with the yawn to start the note but this time sing directly on a vowel sound rather than with the 'h'. Make sure that you give as many counts to getting louder as you do for getting softer. This is a very important part of the exercise.

Do you remember the palm of the hand? You probably thought you had removed all tension as soon as you slightly released the thumb over the fingers – this was not so and neither is it in this exercise. It is essential for your vocal strength to be able to control the voice in both directions and beginning to recognise and understand the tension necessary between both the muscle and the ligaments within the vocal mechanism. Anybody can get louder – getting softer is the difficult bit! Can you work out why? Talk to your singing teacher about this.

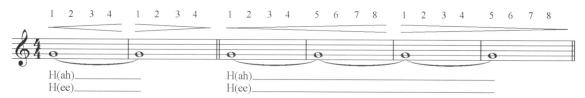

This exercise will develop a greater sense of vocal control and allow you to understand differences in dynamics from soft to loud singing. Remember that it is important to keep in pitch when getting louder so take care with this aspect of the exercise.

Warm-up 8: Scales

Try not to worry about the highest and lowest notes. Keep an even sense of support throughout the exercise. This will eventually develop your strength and extend your vocal range. As noted previously, it is important to develop the high notes in order to give you greater potential as a singer and to increase your personal repertoire.

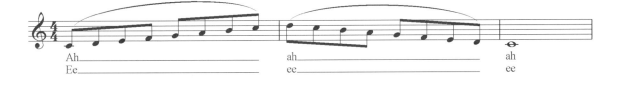

Warm-up 9: Staccato singing on arpeggios

Begin the exercise with the yawn effect but this time allow each note to be sung with a silent 'h'. Use the five vowels identified at the beginning of this section. If you want to check that you are technically correct when singing this exercise, look at yourself in the mirror and notice the position of your larynx when you sing high- or low-pitched notes. At the moment it should remain in a slightly low position. Again, this is something to talk to your teacher about when you have spent some time monitoring your own singing work.

Use as little breath as possible on each note and concentrate on the vowel rather than the 'h' before each note. Try to keep each note equal in both weight and effort. Maintain a sense of light laughter in the work. This is an excellent warm-up exercise because it increases agility in the voice, gives good breath control as well as enables you to gain confidence in pitch and vocal range. As in all these exercises, aim for an easy, free-flowing production of sound and volume. Try both of these exercises:

Finally try this exercise by maintaining a nice light vocal touch to each separate note. This exercise will give you a bright sound and give energy to your singing work.

Nay nay nay nay nay nay nay nay nay nay nay nay nay
Zay zay zay zay zay zay zay zay zay zay zay zay zay

Cool-down exercises

Having completed your workout, it is essential that you cool down your voice to avoid damage and to allow the now-excited laryngeal muscles and the vocal cords to return to a more normal state.

Lip buzzing:

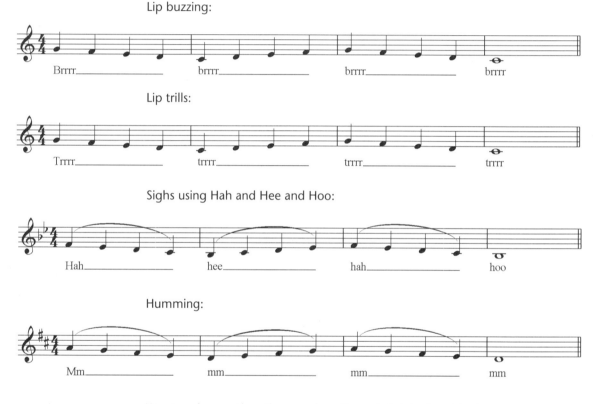

Brrrr_____ brrrr_____ brrrr_____ brrrr

Lip trills:

Trrrr_____ trrrr_____ trrrr_____ trrrr

Sighs using Hah and Hee and Hoo:

Hah_____ hee_____ hah_____ hoo

Humming:

Mm_____ mm_____ mm_____ mm

You can also use the other nasal continuants 'n', 'ny' and 'ng'.

Reflection on the actual warm-up

You will discover that the best types of warm-up vocal exercises are a selection of those that allow the voice to execute:

- easy movement from one note to the next (slides),
- lip and tongue trills,
- scales with a variety of chosen open and closed vowel sounds such as:
  ee [as in b**EE**n] – eh [as in **E**ffort] – ah [as in sp**A**] – aw [as in s**AW**] – oo [as in b**OO**t]
  and

- staccato and legato exercises based on arpeggio figures.

If you feel tired after your warm-ups, then you need to make sure that you are doing the warm-up exercises correctly. However, some of this tiredness might be caused by the fact that you are not used to employing these muscles and after an hour or so the stress will go away. If you continue with a regular but thoughtful practice schedule, you can be assured that your vocal skills will develop and your voice will become much stronger.

It is important to understand that there is a great difference between tiredness and overall fatigue and this is where you will need to consult with your professor and vocal teacher for more personal detail regarding your own vocal issues.

As learning to sing might be a new regime for you, we are aware that pointing out possible signs of vocal fatigue could be alarming. In order to help you at this early stage in your career, it might be worth noting any differences in your daily regime and keep a record for further discussion with your vocal teacher. Answers to the following questions, regarding any changes in your daily routine, might be useful for you to consider as a basis for discussion and consultation:

- Do you drink more water?
- How would you describe your sleep patterns?
- At what times do you eat during the day? What do you eat?
- Do you find your speaking voice is hoarse in the morning?
- Do you find your voice dry in the morning?

If you find any of these factors have changes since you started the serious study of singing, it would be sensible to consult your voice teacher, who will be able to recommend the appropriate action to be taken. Remember that when dealing with the voice, you are exposing your inner body, and so the signals are there for all to witness – that includes your friends, teachers and, most important of all, your audience.

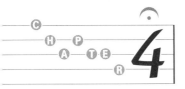

Words, Words, Words

In this chapter we shall be considering one of the most powerful ways in which human beings communicate with each other: through **words.** As performers we need to remind ourselves that words are by no means our only mode of communication: we supplement words with gestures, facial expressions and our chosen proximity to the people we are addressing. At times we replace words altogether, but the fact remains that language is our major tool of thought and expression and without it we would feel impoverished and deprived of part of ourselves.

When we begin to work on a musical in detail, it is almost certainly the **words** that we encounter first. We may know some of the tunes but even these will have a title or some words that make them unique or familiar. For example, how often have you said 'Climb Every Mountain' as a means of encouraging yourself or someone else?

If we are to understand the use of words in a musical, it is necessary to reflect on how we use the spoken word.

Why speak?

Here are some of the ways in which we use words:

To influence others

To plead

To avoid hurting someone

To insult

To express excitement

To express sorrow

NOW:

1. Supply further examples of your own in the box below.

2. Look at a song you are currently working on and decide how the words are used to create the required dramatic impact and intention

Dialogue

In his very entertaining book *Murderers and Other Friends* (1995), the playwright John Mortimer provides some rich insights into how he approached the writing of libretti for works of Musical Theatre. The 'book' or libretto of a Musical is much like a play script when it takes the form of people talking, and, as in real life, the conversation is often fragmented, incomplete, evasive and full of clichés. Characters frequently avoid what they really want to say, struggle to express themselves and sometimes say precisely the opposite to what they actually mean. The true meaning of what they intend to say lies in what we call the 'subtext', and the audience is left to fathom this out by observing the characters' actions.

Why sing?

When John Mortimer came to write the words for arias (or songs, as we would call them in a musical), he realised that this was a very different experience from writing normal dramatic dialogue.

He discovered that, when a character moves into a song, the idea of subtext takes on a new dimension because it comes to the surface and the verbal expression becomes direct, expressive and unambiguous.

For John Mortimer (195–6), 'what is sung is what we all feel beneath the flat and polite surface of our lives ... the aria [or song] is the subtext of our trivial conversations ... we are spared the chat about the weather and the traffic information ... the tenor or soprano within us all and struggling to get out, is released'. 'So', says Mortimer, 'our deepest feelings, but not our spoken comments, easily translate into operatic numbers'. Precisely the same is true for all Musical Theatre.

Question: How do we as performers contribute to the creative process?

Answer: As a performer you bring the language of both words and music into a heightened perception.

Approaching the text

'I am sorry I really didn't mean that ...!'

How many times in conversation have you made this comment? In performance we do not have the opportunity of addressing the audience and questioning whether they understood our interpretation. You have to be strong in your opinions and thoughts about the narrative journey so that your understanding is communicated to everyone listening and seeing your work. This is a huge responsibility for us as performers and is the main thrust of our work as actor-singers. We cannot blame others (lyricist/composer) for not effectively communicating the thoughts through the text of the song. It is our responsibility to become involved in the process and so contribute to the relationship that has already been created, albeit a while ago. It is not often that an actor-singer has the opportunity to talk to the composer and lyricist in person and discuss intimate details about the score and text. We have to use our intellect and power of communication to the ultimate heights in order to be effective in our presentation of the song. So when you communicate in speech or song ask yourself:

- Were you trying to resolve an argument or situation by taking the blame?
- Did you mean what you said?
- Was this a complete mistake and error of judgement?
- Was this just a case of saying the wrong words at the wrong moment?
- What actually happened and why?
- Can you analyse the events and why you said these words?
- Is this really like you?
- Have you ever done this before? If so, why and what are you going to do about it?
- Do you want to do something about it?

In the same way that you can be misunderstood in a simple conversation, so can you in performance. However, in conversation, you have many opportunities to convince others of your real situation. In performance, you do not. The audience listen and make decisions about everything you do! You have to be certain that you are in control of your art and realise that once you place yourself in the spotlight you are there to be judged. You have to be the Olympic athlete in terms of technique and strength of character and you also have to come first in the race as far as your skill and talents are concerned. We have no second chance as actor-singers to establish a relationship with our audience.

Preparing your portfolio

As you will be required to create a portfolio of songs, as part of your studies, you will be undertaking the research necessary to understand the context of the songs chosen. In order to perform these songs, it is appropriate for us to offer you some guidance on how to prepare for this aspect of your work.

Here are two methods of approaching the same work:

- The **first** is for any student who is preparing a single song from a musical.
- The **second** is for any actor who has been chosen to **play the entire role**.

You, as a student, should follow the **same** rules for both, but when preparing a single song from a musical perhaps you should be **even more adventurous** in your research and bring something extra to the work so that you can develop your own acting skills and be creative within the neutral performance space.

Although you must be aware of the musical and the context of the song within it, do not let this knowledge have complete control over your creative impulses, especially when working as a student of this craft.

First method: In order to work on an **individual song** from a musical to develop your strengths as an actor-singer for (i) class, (ii) recital or (iii) cabaret performance, you still have to do the work and **research the world of the character, as observed in the musical itself; you must research the complete musical in order to:**

- **understand the world of the play** so that you recognise the dramatic situations and conflicts faced by the character. If you decide to change the circumstances, such understanding is still essential if the meaning of the song is to be retained.

Example

'I Dreamed a Dream' from *Les Misérables* has past memories in the lyric '. . . Of times gone by . . .'; this is so often misinterpreted as a sad song because these times no longer exist, but the truth of the song is in the fact that there is something to hold on to in life and that is the dream. Why, for example, is the American dream so important to a whole nation? Students tend to read the words on a simplistic level and do not interrogate beneath the surface in order to discover the truth and meaning of the complete thought process. This is why research is so important.

- **recognise the social conditions in which it was written** and then readjust to make the text work for your own personal circumstances. You cannot presume you know what the song is about until you have researched the actual context of the lyric.
- **have knowledge of why the characters feel the way they do** and then allow this to become a relevant part of your own expressive interpretation.
- **have factual information concerning the social restrictions and beliefs and how these impact upon the individual and those surrounding them** and then use this to reinforce and reinterpret your version of the lyric so that it means something to you in the performance space.
- **understand the style of work** and then if you chose to change the style for whatever reasons, you are aware of what went before – always have respect for the original writing and accept that your version is an 'arrangement' in order to give a sense of originality to the work.

Example

Change for change's sake is not good – there will always be many reasons for a change of tempo. When Sandy Shaw performed her song 'Puppet on a String' recently, her performance was totally unlike her approach when she won the Eurovision Song Contest with that song. Then, it was breezy and almost inconsequential, but now it was slow, thoughtful and suited to an older woman reflecting on her past. Another example of this is a recent recording made by Petula Clarke of a hit made famous by her in the 1960s' 'Downtown'. On her latest album sung at the age of 80, she has reinterpreted the song, and it has, yet again, a more reflective tone and a greater sense of inner truth in comparison with the earlier much more 'uptempo' version.

- **recognise the implications for the actor in terms of physicality, vocal work and relationships** and develop these to suit the style of presentation you wish to employ. Remember you need to embrace the physicality of each song you sing within a group of songs. All too often, singers fail to recognise the importance of this, and so all songs sound the same no matter who wrote them.
- **We live in the twenty-first century, while these characters are from an earlier** century – what personal qualities and skills can you bring to this work to illuminate the thoughts of both composer and lyricist?

Things to do

Perhaps for some fun it would be good to see how many versions of the same song you can find and analyse the difference between them. Same words, same music, same performer, different performers – what happens when the words are sung?

Second method: To understand the **character**, as observed in the musical itself, you must research the complete work in order to:

- understand the world of the play
- recognise the social conditions in which it was written
- have knowledge of why the characters feel the way they do
- have factual information concerning social restrictions and beliefs and how these impact upon the individual and those surrounding them
- understand the style of work
- recognise the implications for the actor in terms of physicality, vocal work and relationships
- deal with the fact that we live in the twenty-first century whereas these characters may be from the nineteenth or twentieth century

Something to think about?

When starting to learn to sing in Musical Theatre, there is always a temptation to 'copy' the artiste who has performed the role in the actual show by listening to what are called 'cast recordings'. There is a tendency amongst voice teachers to dissuade students from listening to these and to encourage them to form their own opinions and ideas about the songs. The problem is that it is felt that there is an element of cheating if students are encouraged to listen to previous performances, copy what they hear and so, in effect, learn the song from a perspective other than their own. The claim is often made that imitation is not a good model for learning.

But there is a compromise here to be considered: especially for those in their first year of studies who have little access to 'live' music performers and perhaps have no instrumental skills of their own. This involves **focused** and **critical listening**.

The most important factor in this learning process is to try to avoid the pure repetition and imitation of the vocal qualities of the performer in the recording.

There is, in fact, little chance that you will succeed in imitating perfectly every nuance of the performance heard and admired. Surely, it would not be your intention to create a precise copy of a performance that already exists?

It is perfectly acceptable to learn from the mastery of others but do not deceive yourself as to where the ideas originate from. Always remember the journey and who influenced you in your performance and why! To look at the work of others is an admirable educational activity. Students copy the works of artists in order to observe their own abilities. Creative writers often imitate the works of great writers in order to develop their own inimitable style. Dancers watch and observe the movements of their peers in order to establish similar qualities in their own dance. Never will they replicate the exact detail of the artist being observed and studied.

You should note at this stage that you might be aiming too high. Often performances on CD are the product of many 'takes' and so the actual heard performance never really happened! Our advice here is to be patient and use everything around you to develop your own natural performance. If listening helps you to achieve a secure performance, then that has produced a positive outcome. Just try not to copy without knowing what you are doing and why.

Let us see how you could benefit from listening to other performances in a focused and critical way.

Tasks to support focused and critical listening

- Find or download a copy of the sheet music to follow at the same time as you listen to the recording. (In this way you can start to recognise and link the ideas expressed in the recording with those discovered on the written page.)
- Look at the separate thoughts expressed in the recording and try to find the similar phrases in the vocal score. Are they the same? What do you notice, if they are different?
- What emotions are being expressed throughout the song? Are there changes that you are able to recognise? Why are they there? What do you think the artist achieves by making these decisions?
- Look at the vocal lines and see how the melody moves up and down. Can you recognise where the climax of each phrase is by listening to it?
- Are there any moments when the artist 'goes off book': changes the pitch or does something that is not in the score? Why did they do that?

Having done this and analysed the performance, you must then bring your own ideas to the work when you start to learn to sing the song to which you have been listening. However, it is important that in the early stages of your studies, you **learn the process of singing a song**, not just how to **perform the song**. That comes much later. Rather than relying on the principle of listening to other artists, you could try to focus on learning a song primarily by using your **acting skills** and by doing so develop an intimate and personal understanding of the lyric that you will be responding to.

Here is one suggestion and method of learning which we would encourage you to adopt:

Take any song and write out the lyrics as continuous prose.

It is important to remember that the song communicates thoughts, wishes, desires and emotions and is often spoken (sung) in reaction to received words, memories or passive thoughts or as a direct result of actions by others or self.

Let us look at these words and identify the meanings.

This is sometimes difficult because you are not actually aware that you do not understand the full meaning of a word. This is why it is necessary to research the context of each word and be secure that your thinking is accurate. You need to be able to work below the surface of each word and not just replace one word with another. There needs to be a sense of exploration and research as to why a word has been used and placed in that context. If you can make little sense of the lyric after such work, then you are at least aware of its limitations and of its quality.

For example, if you find a lyric containing the word 'like', this could be replaced with such words as enjoy/love/similar. How many other words can you find to explain 'like'? Now try to find sentences and examples of where 'like' is an option.

Process in action

The preparation of a song and the understanding of the lyric should have integrity, commitment, intelligence, research and a willingness to discover the unknown. First, you must actively try to find a copy of the vocal score of the song to be studied – this might be done by going to the library or downloading the score from the Internet. If you really cannot find the vocal score, we would recommend at this early stage that you find another song. This then gives you an opportunity of seeking guidance from others to help you understand the musical content and perhaps being able to pick out the melody on a keyboard instrument. (See our 'Geographical Tour of a Vocal Score' for help.)

Here we are using as an example a simple folk song entitled 'O Waly, Waly' (vocal score to be found on **page 70**).

First version: Write the lyric out in continuous prose with no punctuation.

The water is Wide I cannot get o'er and neither have I wings to fly give me a boat that will carry two and I will row my love and I.

Second version: Now add breath marks (/) where you feel you need to breathe whilst still making sense of the words and thoughts. Remember that every stop is a hindrance to continuous thought and so raises unnecessary questions in the minds of both the speaker and listener. Try not to overuse the pause for so-called dramatic effect at this point in the work. That comes much later when you really understand the performative value of silence. At sight we often tend to take too many pauses and allow our habitual short patterns of speech to interfere with the poetic flow of the writing.

The Water is Wide/ I cannot get o'er/ and neither have I wings to fly/ give me a boat that will carry two/ and I will row my love and I.

Third version: Look at the original lyrics and punctuation and see how they differ or, for that matter, are similar. Take the final version that follows and make any observations that you feel have an impact upon the mind of the speaker/singer. Note that in the second version the actor-singer has observed the majority of the structure as intended and identified in the third version but has failed to make lines 3–4 a continuous thought.

Line 1. The Water is Wide, I cannot get o'er

Line 2. And neither have I wings to Fly.

Line 3. Give me a boat that will carry two

Line 4. And I will row my love and I.

You might now be thinking – 'well if it is nearly the same, why didn't I just go along with what was written and sing it as it is? Why bother to do all this work?'

The answer is that by exploring the natural reaction to the words you have discovered that the character speaking does not employ the same vocal patterns as yourself. You now know why the song is written like this and you have made an active contribution to the actual process undertaken by engaging with the work of both the lyricist and composer. You have entered their world and shared their creative decisions. You are now an integral part of the creative process and no longer will you see this as 'just a simple folk song'.

You must also be able to speak the text as a dramatic monologue.

In order to do this, you must take yourself through a variety of exercises to achieve a thorough approach to the lyric and the situation. You must make each song your own and sing as if you had written and conceived the words as a result of your own intimate experiences and achievements within this complex, confusing and sometimes disturbing world.

A word of warning: there will sometimes be editorial interference with certain lyrics resulting in changes of punctuation and even of words. In our version of this specific song, the word at the start of the 3rd line is 'Give' whereas in another version it is 'Build'. Clearly the use of one word rather than another gives a completely different meaning and feeling to the intentions of the song. It is up to you as an actor-singer to honour the word given and to interrogate the meaning as something that will affect your performance and thought process.

Reflection on the process – Have you achieved the following?

- Looked at the neutral lyric (no punctuation and pauses given)
- Spoken the words with care and understood each one in turn
- Done your research and discovered a clear picture of how these words are structured
- Given a sense of energy and purpose to the speaking of each word
- Noted where you have started to take breaths and where you feel the phrase ends
- You are now beginning to make sense of the lyric for your own intimate and personal interpretation.

Short interlude

When you have achieved this level of work, it is useful to return to the original writing of the lyric and see where the actual punctuation marks are.

- Is the punctuation different from what you have inserted and if so why?
- What is the lyricist trying to say that you didn't?

- Did you and the lyricist agree on every point? That would be a rare but wonderful experience.

You will have entered the world of the writer and have shown that you have sympathy for the thoughts being expressed: you are now as one! This may be the beginning of a lasting and beautiful relationship between you and this writer. Perhaps more songs will have the same impact upon you as you grow and develop an understanding of this art form.

Now you have the lyric and its meaning secure in your thoughts, and before you look at the melody and the accompaniment you need to find a way of preparing for the lesson that is possibly only in a few days' time.

Discover the internal rhythm of the text

This aspect is very rewarding and involves experimentation and, probably, making mistakes. We can always be sure that the road to artistry is littered with errors of judgement until the truth is discovered and secured by our own intellectual powers.

You may have been fortunate to have had a teacher who inspired you to speak verse, you may have studied the plays of Shakespeare or you might still be fascinated by the use of words in our language. No matter what your background, from now on, words are to be seen as a vital aspect of all your thinking and decision-making. Even if you are not aware of it, our everyday language has much in common with the language of Shakespeare and his treatment of verse together with his use of the familiar iambic rhythm – alternate weak and strong stresses.

To <u>be</u> or <u>not</u> to <u>be</u> . . .

If <u>mu</u>sic <u>be</u> the <u>food</u> of <u>love</u> play <u>on</u>

The moment you are asked to speak the text of a song you are entering the world of the poet, and so you need to be aware of this world and its freedom and constraints. You also need to enjoy the freedom that you can celebrate before returning to the demands of the original creators of the song. This is the moment when you bring your charisma and talent to the creative table.

A song lyric is poetry not just because it has the potential of being set out in order and metrical patterns but for more important reasons such as:

- You are now speaking the text out loud and so you will be heard by others – the art form is becoming public (as it was intended), not intimate.
- There is a possibility that you will give some words extra emphasis and power in order to create a certain image.
- One image that never fails to alert our senses is the word 'fly': it is such a powerful and liberating image. Imagine where you are – on top of a cliff wanting to fall to the ground below, or perhaps by a huge vast expanse of water to be carried by the wind to a more pleasant place; give yourself to nature: embrace the elements, enjoy these images and any emotions they inspire. We remember talking to students one day about the power and magic of the word 'fly' and were so moved that we asked a colleague to write a close harmony arrangement of the pop song 'I Can Believe I Can Fly'

in order to demonstrate how the image is used in all music and at all levels of emotional engagement. There were tears in the house when we sang it!
- You may be caught up in a definite pitch of delivery.
- You may discover an underlying rhythm within the text – it might be both regular and irregular. How will that impact upon your thoughts whilst speaking the words out loud?
- By speaking the words repeatedly until they become second nature, you will discover the intimate qualities of the 'voice' of the character/writer. This discovery can only come from working the text by speaking the words aloud in such a thorough and detailed manner. There are no short cuts in this work!
- You might find a pattern of words which encourages you to punctuate in a certain manner.

If you discover any of these things when speaking your lyrics (having neutralised the text and before putting the song to music), then you are completely 'in the moment' of the thought processes being communicated by the writers and on their wavelength. Remember at this point that we are not speaking verse but accepting that the words have power, rhythm, vocal inflection and above all a sense of melody.

We have to bridge the process between creating the dramatic monologue and identifying the original thoughts of the speaker by redirecting these words into some form of rhythmic metrical pattern that allows the original creative thoughts to be respected and understood.

Try the following exercise once you have experimented with speaking the words out loud, attempting to find patterns and rhythms within the writing.

Set up a clicking pattern allowing each syllable to be given equal time. Do not allow variety between strong and weak beats. Give each syllable equal emphasis until you have broken down the rhythm of the line.

The water is wide, I cannot get o'er
And neither have I wings to fly.

Now set up a pattern of 4 solid beats and tap 1–2–3–4 and aim to get the line to fit into these 4 beats. You will discover a pattern similar to the one below:

The	*wa –*	*ter*	*is*	*wide*	*i*	*can*	*not*	*get*	*o'er*
–	1	–	–	2	–	–	3	–	4

and	*nei –*	*ther*	*have*	*I*	*wings*	*to*	*fly.*	*–*	
–	1	–	2	–	3	–	4	–	

Then start to let the words have a rhythm of their own over a beat. Eventually, you will discover that some words are to be spoken faster to fit in with the strong beats.

If you do this as an experimental aspect of your work, you need reach no conclusion other than the fact that you are aware of an internal rhythm in the text that might be used by the composer to communicate the thoughts of the character. This will give you an added perspective and provide you with a point of discussion with yourself as to why the composer chose to strengthen a specific word. You are now communicating with the minds of these two collaborators (composer and lyricist) at a high level of artistry.

What to do with the actual musical score?

Now that you have tackled the rhythm of the words, you can look at the musical score and start to look at the actual writing and the shapes on the page. Again it is essential that you ask lots of questions. The trick is what questions to ask. You should at all times try to be your own teacher. Never wait to be told – experiment and discover for yourself no matter how costly in terms of your personal time.

Do not forget to consult our **Geographical Tour at the end of this book if you need additional help**.

From looking at the musical score, can you tell whether the singer starts at the first section of the song? If not, what happens before you sing?

Where on the first page does the first word get sung?

See how many times the singer starts and stops in the first few pages and note how long the thoughts are that are being expressed.

Speak each one of them and see if there are any patterns in length or rhythm, etc.

You won't always know if you are correct but it is good to try to see what happens. Remember you are on your own and, as we reminded you in Chapter 1, preparing for a performance can sometimes be a very lonely activity. But it is you that has to prepare for your lesson – no one else can be part of that process.

Having looked at the number of phrases and marked them up on the music and noted whether you sing immediately or later, you are now aware of the structure of the song and probably you can see where repeated phrases come within that structure. Do you notice any similar patterns when singing certain words? These might be clues for the future.

The art of using a pre-recorded piano accompaniment (published, recorded or personally prepared)

The art of using an accompaniment CD comes into play here. We are now fortunate that the industry has advanced so much that we can save ourselves a fortune on professional fees by buying or downloading accompaniments of most songs in the Musical Theatre repertoire. This will certainly be true of any song that you might choose to sing in the first two years of your studies.

If a song is not available with a piano accompaniment, then you could play it yourself, ask a friend to play the melody for you or, if you are lucky, ask a pianist to play the entire accompaniment while you record it on your mobile, iPad or another form of recording equipment.

However, if there is no CD accompaniment, or more importantly a published score for the song you wish to sing, then don't waste time and emotional energy worrying about it. Take action: persuade someone to help you, play the melody for you or, if all fails, change your mind and find another song where there is a published vocal score and at least one version of the song recorded by a reliable artist! So often a lack of initiative, adventure and commitment is used as an excuse for avoiding the work to be done for class and for your teachers.

Whenever possible, you must prepare in a positive and efficient manner for all your classes and never have the '...dog ate it...' excuse! You cannot go to class with the excuse that you don't know the melody because no one would play it for you. It is up to you to do the necessary study in advance. Perhaps this is the moment for you to take time out and learn how to recognise the notes on the piano. Being able to read the notes on the treble clef even if you cannot get the rhythm correct is a great bonus when life gets difficult. This is your journey and you must take responsibility for your own work.

How to listen effectively to the piano accompaniment

Have a copy of the published vocal score with you from the beginning of this learning process. Listen and try to follow *either* the vocal line on the purchased score (follow the words if you can't read the music) *or* the accompaniment depending on the type of CD you have at your disposal. As you listen, concentrate on capturing the mood and essence of the lyric and see where the actual words fit in to the beats and patterns within the music. Then compare your findings with your original thoughts about the song. Note the differences and ask yourself **why** they are different.

Now try to be a voice-over artist as if speaking for a film or a documentary with the piano accompaniment to colour your speaking performance. Imagine that you are using the accompaniment as a film track supporting you speaking over the soundscape. Aim to keep vibrant images in your mind (remembering all that you have already thought about) and allow the music and the words to have some sense of organic continuity.

Remember that if you have already agreed that the song doesn't start immediately, see if you can find a suitable time to begin speaking and then, eventually, singing the song. Look at the score and see if you can count the number of bars before the song starts.

Do this a couple of times so that you become comfortable with the pace of the lyric and the actual music associated with the lyric.

At this point the exciting work really begins.

Imagine that you have written the words of this song and you have heard the music of the accompaniment. Now you want to try to create a melody for this song over the top of the accompaniment with which you are now familiar.

Aim to sing vocal phrases and capture the spirit of what is already there. Do this several times until you are totally comfortable with the phrases.

Have I done enough for my next lesson?

Now is the time to listen to a performance of the song with the published vocal score at hand in order that you can capture the few details in the melody that you might not have understood. You should listen several times to the recording and now you should be very comfortable not only with the style of the song but also with the demands of the vocal line.

How much difference is there between your original version and the one you are now singing? You might be very surprised.

Compare your performances and attempts, and, if you have time, record ·each event and carefully monitor your own journey. If you do this, you will be prepared for any eventuality in the singing class, and your teacher will be able to put the finishing touches to your work and give you those secrets that have eluded you during the last few days of study.

Having explored the song you are probably still not fully aware of how faithful you are to the original intentions of the writers. This is now the time to take it to your teacher in order to put the starting blocks of a performance together to support the work you have already undertaken. Remember that, at all times, you are 'acting through song' and that your teacher/director may well use terminology from the discipline of acting as in the extended example we are now providing. Study it very carefully.

[*This is a transcript of a teaching session, which actually took place one cold November afternoon recently in the presence of both authors and our editor, with Luke from London College of Music. It concerns the performance of the previously mentioned folk song 'O Waly, Waly'.*]

DH: First would you speak the verse with a clear sense of articulation and do not try to act or make sense of the words – ignore the punctuation. Give each word equal weight and clarity.

DH: Well done. What did you discover from this style of delivery?

Luke: I sensed a free but strong vocal power. It was strange as each word appeared to have the same emphasis and weight. It made me respond to the text in a very emphatic, strong and secure way. There was no hesitation in my mind as to why I spoke the words. I did not speak with my usual habitual speech pattern of short passages of text, I just kept going. That made it exciting as if I was out of control and leaning forwards.

DH: Good work and some interesting physical responses to the speaking of the text. Take care that the leaning forwards does not overpower your physicality. Now feel a solid rhythmic beat which we [the class] will clap and you must try and speak with the same energy but attempt to give the words a natural rhythm and flow. This time did you notice anything extra?

Luke: Yes, I felt as if the words had energy and in such words as water the 2nd syllable was given more power than just remaining as a neutral vowel and an 'uh' sound. This was even more noticeable in the speaking of the word 'cannot' – again I felt as if I was slightly desperate in my wishes in reflection of the negative aspect of the opening two lines. The resolution in the 3rd and 4th lines was amazing to speak because it was like a dark cloud lifting from my mind – a solution to the problem.

DH: Very interesting. Thank you for those observations. It is true that text has an amazing power and even in the simplest of folk songs there is a lot to extract from the context of the lyric and the narrative. Well done!

Now in terms of the situation and character can you tell me whether you are alone speaking thoughts to yourself or directing these thoughts to someone else?

Luke: To myself?

DH: OK, if you feel that then speak it as if you are talking to yourself. Remember that you are a person as well. Address yourself with some real intention.

When talking to yourself what happened to the quality and variety of your speaking voice?

Luke: It was very interesting. Clearly I was happy to talk to myself in the opening two lines of the verse. I am summing up the situation. However, the active verb 'give' was not so easy to handle and I think I changed focus a little because I became uncertain as to whether I was speaking to myself or to somebody else – I was not prepared for that idea to come into my mind.

DH: Oh my goodness you have experienced a change of focus within the song already. [*We have always tried to remind students at the early stages of this work to keep things simple. Whether it be text or action be direct and to the point!*] If you were to do this how would you now react?

Luke: Say it to someone who might be able to help!

DH: So are you suggesting that you want to speak the first two lines on your own and then someone comes on stage to be with you?

Luke: No that is too complex and the audience won't understand it unless I have another actor to help me.

DH: So in order to keep the situation simple what do you have to consider?

Luke: That I am singing all 4 lines to someone else or they are present and know that I am there. They might not always hear my thoughts but they are present with me. Oh, how do I do that?

DH: Don't worry, you are actually making the situation simpler and easier to communicate, not more complex. This is fine as at least now all 4 lines allow you to have the same purpose and direction. Speak it to someone who can help you. [*Luke speaks the text carefully and indicates another person on stage but shows little sense of why the words have to be spoken. Needs a greater sense of objectivity and intention.*]

I think we need to define who you are speaking to?

Luke: A boat builder.

DH: [*Laughter (from class)*] And what makes you think he is going to give you a boat without paying for it especially as you don't intend to come back – well not for a while anyway. [Think of the words.]

Luke: Ah good point. Why is it important?

DH: If you know who you are singing to then you know why you are speaking to them as well. This makes the work more interesting. Perhaps we should say that in order to make the action interesting it cannot be straightforward. That is not dramatically interesting. There must be an obstacle otherwise you just get what you want without a fight! That is boring . . .

Luke: Help me! I am totally confused . . .

DH: Never worry about being confused but always try to find a solution despite the consequences. There is always an answer. Let us suggest for the sake of argument that this director has decided on a set of what Stanislavsky called 'given circumstances' for this lyric, such as the location, time period and the actual nature of the situation to be established within the scene. Difficult as it maybe, you as the actor-singer must accept the director's changes as the given circumstances of the play. Acting can then be considered as improvising within a framework of given circumstances. This often needs to happen when treating a song as a complete dramatic scene. If, as director, I were to suggest that you were singing these words to your father and you were his only son what might be the consequence of this text?

Luke: Oh I see. My father has a boat which he needs. I am in love with a girl and I want to be with her rather than stay with my father . . . [*Sudden thought*] I am asking him to give me his boat without a guarantee of returning home. This is my action and the obstacle is that my father will have to sacrifice something in order for me to achieve this.

DH: Indeed. What is actually happening in the lyric as you are playing it? Remember that every moment in this lyric is based on what has happened in the moment preceding it. Acting within this narrative is dealing truthfully with the other characters on stage in order to pursue your specific goal. What is the dilemma here for the son/lover?

Luke: I am feeling really bad, honestly. I want to be with this girl – that is my objective. I also love my father – the obstacle for me to overcome. I need his [love] and help in order to be with my girl.

DH: Ah now we are talking! The opening two lines now become a sensitive appraisal of the situation which you share with your father and then you take the plunge and ask him to help you as only a father could do, knowing that a sacrifice is to be made. Speak the lyric with this objective in mind now that you understand the moment that you are playing within the action of the scene. Remember that the physical action is crucial in an actor's technique because it is the one thing that you are able to maintain on stage.

Luke: I can see the dilemma being created by my desire to achieve my objective. It was hard to speak the 3rd and 4th lines because I knew how difficult it would be for him to hear my words, let alone speak them. Oh my goodness is this what it is about? I would never have thought so much could be gained from so few lines of a song. Do we have to do this all the time?

DH: Yes, remember that this knowledge is eventually to be your own personal technique. This is what you must do at all times as an actor to work through text, sung or spoken. Now sing the song.

[*Pianist now sits at the piano in readiness to accompany the singer. 'O Waly, Waly' arranged by David Henson.*]

DH: Close your eyes and listen to the piano accompaniment for this verse of the folk song. Capture the mood of the music, the tonality and any sense of melody you can. Try and capture the essence of the accompaniment as if it is a '... song without words'.

[*Singer listens carefully with his eyes shut.*]

O Waly, Waly

Arr. by David Henson

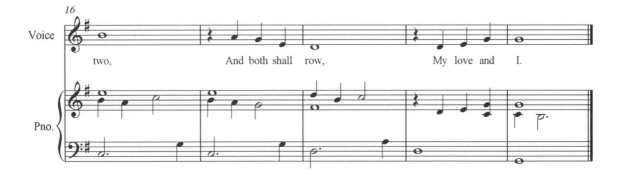

DH: Now listen again.

[*Luke does so and smiles as he appears to be picking out familiar melodic patterns in the accompaniment.*]

DH: Now, today you have a pianist to work for you. In order to make this part of the work happen in your normal working life, you will probably need to prepare the material. However, there will be times when you cannot afford the pianist or want to work on your own. At these times you could prepare for this work by (i) asking a friend to play the melody for you and record it on your mobile etc. or (ii) asking a pianist or tutor to play the accompaniment for you and record as above.

However, today we have a pianist to play for you...

I want you to listen to the accompaniment again and use the music as a subtext for speaking the words. Imagine you are doing a 'voice-over' for a documentary and you are being required to tell the story. You have to fit the words into the musical patterns and end at the same time as the final chord.

[*Luke does this but finds that he speaks the words quite quickly and has to wait a long time for the music to finish.*]

DH: Well done, you spoke the words clearly but you didn't appear to pay much attention to the quality, pace and mood of the music. You also ended far too early. Try it again just being aware that the director of the documentary has required you to speak throughout the music and make the last word connect with the final chord. Think about when to start – perhaps there is an introduction before the words are needed? [Big clue]

[*Again Luke speaks the words but is unable to capture the phrasing.*]

DH: Try again and wait until you think you are given permission to speak by the musical accompaniment.

[*Luke listens carefully and appears to be much more relaxed. He waits a while and then realises that he needs to complete the phrase before speaking. This time the phrases are much more controlled and he has captured the essence of each phrase and the tempo of the thoughts being communicated. He also ends at the same time as the pianist.*]

DH: Bravo!

[*Luke smiles with pleasure...*]

DH: Now for the good bit! I want you to imagine that you are improvising a melody for this song. You have heard the rhythmic and melodic patterns several times, so now use them to support your vocal improvisation. Be brave and sing these spoken thoughts.

O Waly, Waly

Arr. by David Henson

Luke: Are you sure you want me to do this?

DH: Yes. You can't get it wrong because you are improvising your own melody, what could be more liberating than that. Enjoy where your voice takes you. Remember listen for the few thoughts from the piano accompaniment before you start to sing. Use anything that you have heard to help you out…Go for it! You can do it!

[*Luke waits for the introduction to complete and he naturally picks up on the tonality of the harmonic sequences. He uses each thought to express a phrase and he repeats melodic phrases in order to simplify his task. He completes the song a little early but overall, this is a really good effort.*]

DH: I want you to have another try at this song now and have a little more confidence now that you are in control.

[*Luke waits, as before, for the short introduction but this time it appears that he is thinking and anticipating his thoughts. This time he doesn't panic and each phrase is sung with some consistent tone and melodic expression.*]

DH: I honestly wish I had recorded that performance because you actually sung the entire melody of the folk song with accuracy to notation, pitch and pace. You have never been taught what to sing and yet you have now captured the essence of this song. Brilliant work! You should be very proud of yourself. Now if you can do all that on your own – what do you think you can do when you have the assistance of your peers and teachers to help you also?

DH: [*To those watching and listening*] Finally, I then tried a little experiment.

I gave the pianist a copy of two more different arrangements of this same folk song and asked Luke to listen to the accompaniment once and then use his inspiration to sing the melody using these accompaniments.

Reflection on the process

The first version was a simplified version with an accompaniment which started on the first note of the vocal melody and so there was no chance for a thought process before Luke started to sing. Having heard the accompaniment through once, he realised that he had to 'action the thought' immediately and indicate to the pianist when he was ready to sing.

The second version was the well-known arrangement by Benjamin Britten, and once Luke had worked out the pace of the accompaniment and the interesting use of chords to create the soft swelling of the waves in the river, he was able to sing this version with a remarkable degree of confidence. So much was achieved because the understanding of the text was paramount before the music became part of the process. All too often we are encouraged to start with the music and then return to the lyric but by that time it is too late for the artistry to be accessed in an efficient and engaged manner.

You can be certain that if you work at this level your teachers will be so impressed with your achievements that you will want to achieve even more! You will have conquered such a large proportion of the basic work with the sung material that they will want to spend the majority of the class finding out exciting nuances in the musical score and the voice in order for you to achieve the subtleties required for the final performance. What more can you ask for in your studies?

Having achieved a sense of the journey being undertaken in the actual sung text, you will undoubtedly have made some discoveries of your own. These now need to be brought to the actual performance. You must also remember that:

- whilst you are singing you must believe that you are a real person
- the music is your emotional subtext
- all humans have a common set of feelings to express within this work
- if you don't let it show, no one will know what you are thinking
- you are making art
- you are to engage and communicate with your audience
- you must have spontaneity in every moment of the song
- you have to play the detail of what is happening and being thought
- you should never try to repeat what you did in your last performance – always try to create something new

Exploring the text further: Exercises and activities

- Put text into your own words and perform any lyric as a short monologue. Invent a scenario for your lyric. Create a time, place and situation.
- In most songs there is a struggle within the inner person – discover what it is in the lyric chosen for study. What makes the character want to sing and why?
- Who are you singing to, and why, in each melodic phrase?
- Take each phrase within the lyric and make sure you understand every word spoken. Don't take the text for granted. Don't pretend you know what each word means. Make sure you understand.
- In the speaking and eventually the singing of the lyric, you will need to work through opposing forces. Find small obstacles to make the work a little more difficult to achieve: e.g. you may consider yourself to be polished and graceful in manner but in reality you might be innocent, confused and full of unpredictable mood changes.
- Mark all the shifts in the emotional drive within the lyric and mark them out in pencil on the score.
- You might like to find a way to make physical the shifting thoughts by using different movements to indicate phrase lengths and thought patterns. Use

your hands and body to do this! These needn't be included in the final performance – use as a rehearsal exercise.

● Develop a clear idea of the plan (structure) of your song in terms of its emotional journey. Does it have a verse and chorus – how do you deal with this to ensure the emotional journey is maintained?

● A song can be a specific thought, or can recount a story or a dream. Are they passive thoughts, recurring thoughts or active thoughts? Where is the focus of the song?

● Record your performance on video. Play back and turn off the sound and comment on each emotion seen in your whole physicality. Use someone, as an audience, and present to them a silent version of the song. What do they learn from your performance?

● Describe for yourself, in writing, the environment in which you are singing the song. Close your eyes before you begin to sing and describe the images and the detail you have written about. Imagine a DVD of the scene and visualise yourself in the film as it is running in your head.

● Always remember that when doing this work it is up to you how the information is to be received by the audience. It can be whatever you decide.

3 *Understanding the Musical*

5 The Anatomy of the Musical

Musical Theatre is arguably the most popular form of mass live entertainment ever invented, and since it was infiltrated by the film and television industries, it has become a global commodity. For example, even before its release as a film in 2011–2013, *Les Misérables* had been seen by 60 million people worldwide. With its logos and associated merchandise, the modern **musical** has dominated international theatre, so that you are just as likely to see the same shows advertised in Tokyo, Cape Town, Mumbai or Sydney as in the West End or on Broadway.

There are, of course, many forms of Musical Theatre: **plays** with music from the times of the ancient Greeks or the Middle Ages, and certainly works such as *The Beggar's Opera* enable the art form to be considered as a means of entertaining and yet informing the audience of social and political issues. **Operas**, such as those written by Handel or Verdi, and **operettas** by such writers as Gilbert and Sullivan or Franz Lehar are only two examples, but it is the musical, a form that was originally known as **musical comedy**, that has come to be the most popular choice for all age groups. It is this world that you have chosen to enter!

Works of Musical Theatre are the creation of playwrights, **librettists**, **lyricists**, **composers** and **choreographers**, and as Otis Guernsey Jr, the editor of *Playwrights, Lyricists, Composers on Theater* (1960), pointed out, these individuals are all, in a sense, dramatists. As a student and potential practitioner of their work, it is essential that you understand the content, form and structure of what they have written, and this may require some research. You will notice that, when we refer to an entire musical, we use the term 'the work'. This is to distinguish the original work from the piece that emerges in performance, which is sometimes, rather confusingly, called 'the text' by Performance Studies scholars.

Types of Musical Theatre

- Backstage musical: a show that examines and is set in the life of the theatre and its performers. Example: *Kiss Me, Kate* (Cole Porter/S. and B. Spewack).
- Book musical: a musical based on a substantial book or play or having a newly created 'book' of dialogue and lyrics. There will be a strong narrative line and carefully drawn characters. Example: *Oklahoma!* (Rodgers and Hammerstein).

- Concept musical: a show based on a single idea, such as 'work' or events in a day. Example: *Company* (Stephen Sondheim).
- Dance musical: in which the story and mood is established through dance of many styles. This, obviously, is a 'company' show in which all the cast can dance. Example: *Chicago* (John Kander/Fred Ebb and Bob Fosse).
- Jukebox musical: a musical where the music is entirely derived from recorded music taken from a particular period, often the 1950s or 1960s. There have, for example, been musicals based on songs from The Spice Girls, The Beatles, Gerry and the Pacemakers, ABBA and Buddy Holly. Example: *Buddy* (Alan Janes and various songwriters).
- Meta-musical: a musical that moves outside the various traditional forms of Musical Theatre and features bold experiment. Example: *Starlight Express* (Andrew Lloyd Webber/Richard Stilgoe/Don Black/Arlene Phillips).
- Opera: a music drama in which all the dialogue is sung. This form is usually associated with classical music and was once seen as more 'serious' than the musical. However, modern operas and productions of earlier operas now require their performers to sing, dance and act well and will exploit all forms of modern theatre technology. Example: *Salome* (Richard Strauss).
- Operetta: a light-hearted and often humorous work in which there may be both spoken and sung dialogue. Example: *The Pirates of Penzance* (Gilbert and Sullivan).
- Physical theatre: dependent on the physical, acrobatic and circus skills of the performers. Dialogue may be minimal or non-existent and music may well be used to underscore the physicality of the performance. Example: *Street of Crocodiles* (Simon McBurney/Mark Wheatley/Bruno Schulz for Theatre de Complicite).
- Plays with songs: plays in which the action may be punctuated by songs but the majority of the dialogue is spoken. Example: *Mother Courage and Her Children* (Brecht/Weill).
- Revue: a miscellany of songs, sketches and dances often centred on a particular theme. Example: *Set to Music* (Noël Coward).
- Cabaret: an intimate performance of songs and dances staged in a café, hotel or bar and in which the audience may well be eating and drinking. Example: *The Threepenny Opera* (Brecht/Weill).
- Through-sung musical: a musical where the entire action is conveyed through the songs and music. Example: *Les Misérables* (Schönberg/Boublil).

SUGGESTED ACTIVITY

1. Name at least two examples of each kind of musical and list them in the box below.

2. Add at least one song from each type of Musical Theatre (including opera) to your portfolio.

Types of song

Songs from works of Musical Theatre may take many forms: here are descriptions and definitions to assist you in selecting a variety of material.

Ballad: sometimes known as the **show ballad**, this often means a reflective and personal song which reveals the state of mind of a leading character. It may take the form of a 'soliloquy' in drama and will almost invariably be sung to a strong and memorable melody that may be used at other points in the work. There are, in fact, varieties of the ballad which also explore the **narrative** element within the musical and inform the story and progress of the action. Sometimes the purpose of the song is to describe aspects of the action that are not seen by the audience but to indicate a passing of time. For example, in the engaging and evocative song 'Round and Round' from *The Fantasticks*, we embrace the passing of time in a moment of song. This is where the magic of Musical Theatre is at its highest point of expression because words alone cannot continue the action. So the song adds another dimension to the spectacle of the production. Finally, there is the more exciting **dramatic ballad** chosen to explore a high point within the overall structure, but it is often too difficult to replicate outside the context of the actual musical itself.

We often suggest to students considering a Musical Theatre audition that they sing a ballad as one of their choices. The reasons are simple – it requires the singer to be 'in the moment', and the song is direct in terms of its audience and focus, for example, girl to boy, boy to girl or mother to son/daughter. Furthermore, they are often written by the creators of the musical as the 'catch' in the ear – otherwise referred to as the 'earworm' – that nobody can forget as they go out of the theatre. And finally, perhaps most importantly for the audition, the ballad is a song that can usually be sung completely out of context and have a life within the actor-singer's mind. This enables the singer to express a life experience which is easy to create and portray in performance. Sometimes, however, reflection on the past or a dream element are much harder to achieve in an audition where you are trying to engage your audience with your own personality, spirit and energy.

We also suggest that you investigate the heritage of the musical rather than identifying the most recent hit in the West End, buying the score and replicating the performances seen on the stage. So we would encourage you to explore traditional repertoire when considering the examples of each song category.

It is understood that you will naturally identify with contemporary works but only recently we heard students working on a cabaret exploring the musicals of

Rodgers and Hammerstein and saying such things as 'why don't we do more of this: the lyrics and music are great and so intriguing?'

Before starting work on discovering these various song types, perhaps it would be useful to know a little about the purpose of the song. We would suggest that you consider **four** basic categories of song for the time being: (i) narrative – where the song tells a story either personal or plot driven; (ii) didactic – where the song informs the audience about something specific to character or plot; (iii) subjective – where the singer involves the audience in being aware of their personal situation and how they feel about something; and finally (iv) informative – where the song is used to excite the audience's attention and have some connection with the forthcoming outcome within the plot, enabling the audience to engage with the singer and action in a positive manner.

Things to Do:

1. When listening to the examples given and other performances by your peers in class or at the theatre, start to compile a list of songs and identify their main purpose within the musical.

2. When considering a song for your personal portfolio, identify whether the song you heard performed was a good vehicle to display your talent, musical potential, skills as an actor and, perhaps most importantly, your ability to carry the role in a convincing and appropriate manner. Think of these things in consideration of self but also think about them in the work of others.

Consider the following when identifying a song to be suited to yourself or others:

talents of the singer – in terms of vocal range, agility, articulation and clear understanding of style of singing

musical potential of the singer – display good sense of rhythm, focus on relationship with accompanist, subtle phrasing, structure of the writing and ability to keep in pitch

skills as an actor – use the opportunity to communicate effectively emotional and character

ability to carry the role – to be able to control the form and structure of the song and to keep the emotional journey alive throughout the entire song

Such composers as Irving Berlin, Cole Porter, Jerome Kern, Kander and Ebb, Stephen Schwartz, Burt Bacharach, Stephen Sondheim, Jerry Herman and Andrew Lloyd Webber, to name but a few, are all prolific creators of the ballad in its many forms and guises.

Show ballad

Voice	Song title	Show	Composer/lyricist
Sop.	'This Can't be love'	*The Boys from Syracuse*	Rodgers and Hammerstein
Mezzo	'Anyone Can Whistle'	*Anyone Can Whistle*	Stephen Sondheim
Tenor	'All I Care About'	*Chicago*	Kander and Ebb
Baritone/bass	'If I Sing'	*Closer Than Ever*	Shire and Maltby

Other examples might include: 'Time after Time' by Jule Styne, 'Small World' by Sondheim and Styne, 'A Quiet Thing' by Kander and Ebb, 'With Every Breath I Take' by Cy Coleman, 'On the Street Where You Live' by Lerner and Loewe and 'Maria' by Bernstein and Sondheim.

Investigate more songs within this category, listen to recordings, choose the repertoire you are attracted to and place a copy of the score into your portfolio for future use and study.

Narrative ballad

Voice	Song title	Show	Composer/lyricist
Sop.	'My Funny Valentine'	*Babes in Arms*	Rodgers and Hart
Mezzo	'Send in the Clowns'	*A Little Night Music*	Stephen Sondheim
Tenor	'Mack the Knife'	*The Threepenny Opera*	Weill and Blitzstein
Baritone/bass	'How to Handle a Woman'	*My Fair Lady*	Lerner and Loewe

Other examples might include: 'A Good Thing Going' by Stephen Sondheim, 'Poor Jud Is Dead' by Rodgers and Hammerstein, 'Meditation I' by Geld and Udell, 'If I Had a Fine White Horse' and 'Race You to the Top of the Morning' by Simon and Norman and 'Mama, Look Sharp' by Sherman Edwards.

Investigate more songs within this category, listen to recordings, choose the repertoire you are attracted to and place a copy of the score into your portfolio for future use and study.

Dramatic ballad

Voice	Song title	Show	Composer/lyricist
Sop.	'Vanilla Ice Cream'	*She Loves Me*	Jerry Bock
Mezzo	'As Long As He Needs Me'	*Oliver*	Lionel Bart
Tenor	'Being Alive'	*Company*	Stephen Sondheim
Baritone/bass	'I've Grown Accustomed to Her Face'	*My Fair Lady*	Loewe and Lerner

Other examples might include: 'My Name' by Lionel Bart, 'My Husband Makes Movies' by Maury Yeston, 'The Wages of Sin' by Rupert Holmes, 'Joe, Joe' by Working, 'Send in the Clowns' by Stephen Sondheim, 'Glitter and Be Gay' by Bernstein and Wilbur and 'September Song' by Kurt Weill.

When considering the ballad for the purposes of the audition, we would stress the fact that the dramatic ballad is perhaps the least suitable. The main reason for this is that they are songs that identify personal weaknesses, and these have to be indicated by the vocal qualities employed. For example, when singing 'Being Alive' from the musical *Company*, you have to take into account the situation that precedes the song and the dark mood to which Robert, the main character, has to adjust his thoughts and his emotional state in order to be able to begin to sing this song. When it is taken out of context, all too often this song is sung as a power ballad and given a life of its own. This may be magical in itself but not true to the precise dramatic situation within the musical. Accordingly, there is a real danger that your listeners will not be able to understand your emotional journey and will think that the vocal blemishes in the sung line are a sign of weakness rather than a moment of strength, great sincerity and truth. Another song that has similar problems regarding the actual vocal qualities and the dramatic situation is also by Sondheim. This is the song 'Not a Day Goes By' from *Merrily We Roll Along*. This song is sung twice by different characters in completely different dramatic situations and emotional predicaments.

The problems are not insurmountable but the singing of the two songs we have been discussing raises too many 'issues' to be safe songs to sing for an audition. Both of these songs, and many more in this category, elicit a heightened response from the audience and are defined by the nature of the surrounding text. In an audition or assessment, it is difficult to convey the sense that a character has reached a moment when s/he can speak no more and has to sing.

Investigate more songs within this category, listen to recordings, choose the repertoire you are attracted to and place a copy of the score into your portfolio for future use and study.

Character song: may well come from a revue, music hall or musical and will reveal vital aspects of a particular character in the show. It may well be comic or idiosyncratic like 'I'm Just a Girl Who Can't Say No' from *Oklahoma!* and will be performed in a way that is very distinctive and typical of the character performing it. Perhaps we should give a word of warning for when you are seeking songs for the audition portfolio. Often, the character song is so tightly connected to the actual plot that there is little chance of the singer being able to give it a 'new life' and context because of the structure and specificity of the lyric. However, there are plenty of songs that encourage the actor-singer to recreate and consider a variety of contexts. Look out for the lyrical motif in these songs such as the 'I want' (aiming for the future) or 'I am' (singing about now – placed in the present tense – and thus very active in emotional connection with the sung lyric) which clearly indicates the personal journey of the character. The 'I am' factor is well worth considering for an audition as it allows you to have an active thinking process and regard the moment of singing as being the moment of revelation. For example, 'This Is the Moment' from *Jekyll and Hyde* has the authentic sense of immediacy that is suitable for the audition process.

Character song

Voice	Song title	Show	Composer/lyricist
Sop.	'I Feel Pretty'	*West Side Story*	Bernstein and Sondheim
Mezzo	'Miss Byrd'	*Closer Than Ever*	Shire and Maltby
Tenor	'Grow for Me'	*Little Shop of Horrors*	Menken and Ashman
Baritone/bass	'I, Don Quixote'	*Man of La Mancha*	Leigh and Darion

Other examples might include: 'I Am What I Am' by Jerry Herman, 'I Got Rhythm' by George and Ira Gershwin, 'I'm Glad I'm Not Young Anymore' and 'I Could Have Danced All Night' by Loewe and Lerner, 'Miss Marmelstein' by Harold Rome and 'The Lonely Goatherd' by Rodgers and Hammerstein.

Investigate more songs within this category, listen to recordings, choose the repertoire you are attracted to and place a copy of the score into your portfolio for future use and study.

Patter song: is sung like very rapid speech, and the entertainment of such a song often depends on the dexterity with which the performer can communicate the meaning by articulating all the syllables. The works of Gilbert and Sullivan contain many such witty songs, and the many Musical Theatre works of Stephen Sondheim have continued in their footsteps. However, the current influences of popular culture also have a great significance for the musical of today, and the 'patter' element has now been replaced by what we would refer to as 'rap'. To celebrate Sondheim's contribution to this form of song lyric, we have chosen specific examples for his musicals.

Patter song

Voice	Song title	Show	Composer/lyricist
Sop.	'On the Steps of the Palace'	*Into the Woods*	Stephen Sondheim
Mezzo	'The Miller's Son'	*A Little Night Music*	Stephen Sondheim
Tenor	'How I Saved Roosevelt'	*Assassins*	Stephen Sondheim
Baritone/ bass	'Everybody Says Don't'	*Anyone Can Whistle*	Stephen Sondheim

Other examples might include: 'I Can Cook Too' by Leonard Bernstein, 'Another Hundred People' by Stephen Sondheim, 'Drop That Name' by Styne and Comden/Green, 'Why Can't the English' by Loewe and Lerner and 'Words, Words, Words' by John Dempsey and Dana P. Rowe.

Investigate more songs within this category, listen to recordings, choose the repertoire you are attracted to and place a copy of the score into your portfolio for future use and study.

Standard: is a song that may originally have come from a show but has become so well known that it is performed in many other contexts and by a variety of vocalists. Examples would be 'When You Walk through a Storm' from *Carousel* or 'Moon River' from *Breakfast at Tiffany's*. There are many varieties of this type which are identified by their specific rhythmic flavour and character. They mainly have a 'swing' accompaniment and have the potential to suit the many different talents of singers from each decade, and so the song is interpreted in a huge variety of ways. You only have to think of recordings by artists such as Frank Sinatra, Ella Fitzgerald, Michael Buble and Robbie Williams to hear the range of interpretations that are possible. One of the main

advantages of these songs is the fact that they are neither ballads in the true sense of the word (as described above) nor jazzy uptempo numbers, which both require a more distinct technique to make them successful in performance. These are excellent songs to use at the beginning of your journey to enjoy and to develop a useful technique without making too many demands on both your vocal register and your vocal
technique.

Suggested activity

It might be a useful exercise to search the library and other sources for some of the recordings of these 'standards' and trace the backstory for each song. How many different versions can you collect and what are the differences?

Standard

Voice	Song title	Show	Composer/lyricist
Sop.	'Let Me Entertain You'	*Gypsy*	Styne and Sondheim
Mezzo	'Getting to Know You'	*The King and I*	Rodgers and Hammerstein
Tenor	'Nice Work If You Can Get It'	*Crazy for You*	George and Ira Gershwin
Baritone/bass	'Try to Remember'	*The Fantastiks*	Schmidt and Harnick

Other examples might include: 'A Fine Romance' by Jerome Kern, 'From This Moment On' by Cole Porter, 'Let's Face the Music and Dance' by Irving Berlin and such songs as 'Alfie' by Burt Bacharach and 'Put On a Happy Face' by Charles Strouse.

We should consider the **blues** as being a distinct category of the standard despite the fact that as a true song form it is sung by few artistes and is rarely used in a musical. Songs such as 'Black and White' by Coleman and Stewart from the musical *Barnum* and 'Funny Hunny' by Kander and Ebb from *Chicago* are proof of its influence within Musical Theatre, although it is often evidenced more strongly in other songs such as the **uptempo** number. There is also the 'waltz' (captured so magnificently in the works of both Rodgers and Sondheim), which is influenced directly by the 'jazzy' feel and tempo of the 'blues'. However, it is in the **torch song**, the anthem of the main character (often female) revealing the heightened emotion of their individual emotional journey, that we have the great sense of depth associated with the true blues singer and their music. This musical statement is often of a great depth and passion and is the revelation of both agony and ecstasy. It is in these moments that the truth of Musical Theatre reveals its hidden secrets and enables the art form to achieve great heights, but it is also true to say that these moments cannot be taught and have to be matched alone with the religious passion and individuality of the singer.

Uptempo

Voice	Song title	Show	Composer/lyricist
Sop.	'Hello, Dolly'	*Hello, Dolly*	Jerry Herman
Mezzo	'Always True to You in My Fashion'	*Kiss Me, Kate*	Cole Porter
Tenor	'If This Isn't Love'	*Finian's Rainbow*	Lane and Harburg
Baritone/bass	'Seventy-Six Trombones'	*The Music Man*	Meredith Willson

Other examples might include: 'Who Will Buy?' by Lionel Bart, 'New York, New York' by Bernstein and Comden/Green, 'Waiting for Life' by Flaherty and Ahrens, 'No Time at All' by Schwartz and 'Chief Cook and Bottle Washer' by Kander and Ebb.

Waltz

Voice	Song title	Show	Composer/lyricist
Sop.	'One More Kiss'	*Follies*	Stephen Sondheim
Mezzo	'Gorgeous'	*The Apple Tree*	Bock and Harnick
Tenor	'Ten Minutes Ago'	*Cinderella*	Rodgers and Hammerstein
Baritone/bass	'Look Over There'	*La Cage Aux Folles*	Jerry Herman

Other examples might include: 'Find Yourself a Man' by Styne and Merrill, 'Just a Kiss Apart' by Styne and Robin, 'She Is Not Thinking of Me' by Loewe and Lerner, 'Together Forever' by Schmidt and Jones and 'Shall We Dance' by Rodgers and Hammerstein.

Torch song

As it is more difficult to put these songs into vocal categories (for the reasons stated above), here are a few examples: 'My Funny Valentine' by Rodgers and Hart, 'Somewhere over the Rainbow' by Arlen and Harburg, 'Every Time We Say Goodbye' and 'Night and Day' by Cole Porter and 'The Man That Got Away' by Arlen and Gershwin.

- **Duets/trios**: take the form of dialogue between two or three characters. They may include expressions of love or frustration and may involve moments when the voices are heard singly or in unison and harmony with each other. Examples would include the 'marriage' song 'Make of Our Lives' from *West Side Story* as a duet or the trio from *Guys and Dolls*, in which three of the characters hold a sung discussion. Knowing how to relate to the other singer in a duet or trio requires particular and considerable skill.

Duets for two women (soprano/mezzo soprano)

Voice	Song title	Show	Composer/lyricist
Sop./Sop.	'If Mama Was Married'	*Gypsy*	Styne and Sondheim
Sop./Mez.	'Everyday a Little Death'	*A Little Night Music*	Stephen Sondheim
Sop./Mez.	'A Boy Like That'	*West Side Story*	Bernstein and Sondheim
Mez./Mez.	'I Know Him So Well'	*Chess*	Andersson, Ulvaeus and Rice

Duets for two men (tenor/baritone/bass)

Voice	Song title	Show	Composer/lyricist
Ten./Ten.	'Right Track'	*Pippin*	Stephen Schwartz
Ten./Bar.	'Guys and Dolls'	*Guys and Dolls*	Frank Loesser
Ten./Bar.	'I'm Nothing without You'	*City of Angels*	Coleman and Zippel
Bar./Bar.	'Agony'	*Into the Woods*	Stephen Sondheim

Duets for a man and woman

Voice	Song title	Show	Composer/lyricist
Mez./Bar.	'Anything You Can Do'	*Annie Get Your Gun*	Irving Berlin
Mez./Ten.	'Color and Light'	*Sunday in the Park with George*	Stephen Sondheim
Sop./Ten.	'I Could Be Happy with You'	*The Boyfriend*	Sandy Wilson
Mez./Bar.	'Perfectly Marvelous'	*Cabaret*	Kander and Ebb

Trios

Voice	Song title	Show	Composer/lyricist
S/M/M	'Matchmaker'	*Fiddler on the Roof*	Bock and Harnick
S/T/B	'Soon'	*A Little Night Music*	Stephen Sondheim
T/T/B	'Pretty Lady'	*Pacific Overtures*	Stephen Sondheim
S/T/B	'She Loves Me Not'	*Closer Than Ever*	Shire and Maltby

So why do we need this information?

Why is this information of any importance to you as you work on an individual song from a musical? After all, we are asked to sing many songs from musicals but never get a chance to play that character in the entire musical? And why it is essential that you grasp the nature of different styles and traditions of Musical Theatre from the past?

The answer is that this and all the information that we give will greatly deepen your knowledge and understanding and enhance your skills so that any performance you may give will have genuine **authenticity**.

Authenticity, just like the concept of **charisma**, is something on which you and your work will be constantly judged and will form the basis of your future success.

We tend to use the expressions 'authentic' and 'authenticity' in two ways but both meanings have absolute relevance to the work of a performer and must underpin any preparation and presentation of work. We describe a performance as authentic when it comes as nearly as possible to the intentions of the original creator of the work. In the case of music, this may mean playing the piece on an instrument that is exactly like the instrument for which the piece was written and playing it in the style in which it would originally have been performed. Obviously, this can cause problems, because finding or creating such an instrument may be impossible and very expensive or it may not always be easy to find out precisely how the work would have originally sounded. We only have the composer's markings to go on and we often need to rely on historians of performance to help us understand the performance styles of earlier periods. The same is exactly true for works of Musical Theatre. However, if we do not aim to achieve some level of authenticity in our performance of a piece that was written in the past, we can never do it justice. The most important feature of this aspect of authenticity is that we understand the spirit of the original, and in order to do this we do need to know about and understand how, why and in what context a work was created.

But authenticity means much more than an attempt to recreate the original performance style of a work. Indeed, it may mean adopting more modern techniques and approaches. **You can only do this if you initially understand where you are coming from.** For a performance to be authentic, in the best sense of the word, it must be **truthful** and **faithful** to the original intentions of the creator. You, as a performer, must personally engage with the thoughts, ideas, emotions and situations that brought the work into being. You are the medium through which these are shared with an audience.

It follows that you always need a profound understanding and appreciation of what you are working on, and it is for this reason that we are now going to provide you with a brief guide to the varying styles and genres that have emerged during previous decades. This will enable you to place any piece you encounter in Musical Theatre in its context and perform works with genuine dramatic truth.

6 The Origins and Development of Musical Theatre

The musical, as we understand it today, has its origins in the last century but its emergence was greatly influenced by earlier forms of popular entertainment. Social issues, world events and changing fashions all made their impact on the development of Musical Theatre and it is important to understand some of these as you explore the history of the subject you have chosen for your study and possible career.

Let us begin by going back to the years before the twentieth century and consider some of what was happening in the world and in entertainment:

Pantomime	**Pantomime** as we understand it in the UK had its origins in the late eighteenth century as an entertainment that combines singing, dancing, storytelling, comic turns and circus skills. It was, however, in the nineteenth century that it began to assume the form we would recognise today. In the United States, the word pantomime means what the rest of the English-speaking world calls 'mime' and the nearest that the American theatre comes to the British 'panto' is in shows for children's theatre.
	In many English-speaking countries, the annual pantomime is quite likely to be the only live theatrical event attended by large sections of the population and many theatres rely on their pantomime, running from just before Christmas until well into the New Year to finance their activities for much of the year. Because of this phenomenon, many students completing courses in Musical Theatre obtain their first professional jobs in pantomime, and, once it is known that you have completed such training, it is quite possible that you will be approached to direct or contribute to one of the many amateur and community pantomimes that happen every year.
	What is sometimes referred to as 'traditional' panto consists of a well-known fairy story presented in a variety of colourful settings with a great deal of dancing by a chorus, direct address to the audience, slapstick comedy and much 'cross-dressing' with the leading male role played by a woman. This latter convention dates from the time when women played 'breeches parts' and provided audiences with the rare opportunity to see women's legs!

	However, it is much more likely today that the lead roles will be played by actors known from TV 'soaps' and that gender reversals for the 'romantic interest' will no longer be used. Nevertheless, the convention whereby the 'dame' will be played by a man will almost certainly be preserved. The music for pantomimes is invariably drawn from the popular music of the day and, although songs may be taken out of their original context, it is just as important for their performance to reflect their new context. You ignore pantomime as an aspect of Musical Theatre at your peril and it requires a very high level of skill and dedication if it is to 'work' in the theatre; the experience of appearing in a well-directed pantomime is invaluable.
Political, theatrical and social events to be noted	**Pantomime** is a form of popular Musical Theatre that has survived and developed for over 200 years. It has never successfully been transformed into film or TV/DVD format and depends entirely upon live interaction with an audience. When pantomimes were first presented, they were invariably staged in theatres that had a proscenium ('picture frame') stage with a forestage: a combination which was ideal for stage effects, stage pictures and direct address to the audience; theatres of this kind remain ideal for pantomime. The first pantomimes were staged when America was still part of the British Empire (the largest empire the world has ever seen) but the American War of Independence broke that bond. Pantomimes grew in popularity throughout the nineteenth century, a period of enormous changes in technology (including the transition from oil lights to gas and then electric stage lighting) and in attitudes towards women: the growth of railways and the gradual urbanisation of Europe produced a new breed of theatregoers seeking cheap and striking live entertainment. In spite of two catastrophic World Wars in 1914–1918 and 1939–1945, there remained a constant demand for a reassuringly familiar escapist form of theatre and a sense of communal celebration at Christmas, and, for many families, the annual visit to a pantomime became a ritual. With the growth of recording, film and TV, the 'stars' of these media became the latest performers to benefit from pantomime, and this has now been extended to a whole range of 'celebrities'. Pantomime has always thrived on contemporary references and jokes and will probably continue to do so.
Minstrel shows	**Minstrel shows**, which had their origins in the 1830s in the United States, remained one of the most popular types of Musical Theatre both live and, later, on TV well into the 1970s. The first minstrel show was devised by Thomas Dartmouth Rice, a white entertainer who specialised in **patter songs** and who blacked his face in an ironic representation of a black American slave 'Jim Crow'. When Rice visited Britain in 1836, his show, which would now be considered politically incorrect and unacceptable, ensured that this form of entertainment became popular on both sides of the Atlantic. Minstrel shows drew on the rich spoken dialect and song and dance traditions of African Americans and, after their introduction by Rice, were also presented by black performers, who did not hesitate to borrow and lampoon his ideas. However, even when black performers were involved, they were still expected to 'black up' with what had become the

	traditional make-up of very black face and white lips. This sometimes sentimental form of family entertainment usually consisted of a troupe of actor/musicians sitting in a semicircle playing banjos, fiddles and tambourines and 'bones' and singing wistful songs and ballads. Two characters, the **Interlocutor** and the **Bones**, would engage in witty dialogue and backchat interspersed with **soft shoe** dances. By the 1960s and 1970s, this apparently simple formula had developed into the *Black and White Minstrel Show*, which not only was one of the most spectacular, colourful and successful shows in London and on British TV but also provided a stimulus for the increasing use of authentic black music and dance as a basis of new types of Musical Theatre.
Political and social events to be noted	**Minstrel shows** developed as the United States was emerging as an independent nation and a future world power. The energy of the country was typified by the creation of what we would now term 'show business' by such entrepreneurs as Barnum and by a host of inventions and innovations such as the telegraph, vulcanised rubber for boots and tyres and the departmental store. Previously undreamt of consumer goods became available to anyone with the enterprise to pay for them. Some Americans became very rich at the time of the Gold Rush and others simply followed a dream. At the same time, however, minstrel shows grew out of the lingering deprivation and musical sadness of black people and, although the slave trade had been abolished throughout the British Empire, a group of Southern States of America persisted in keeping slaves. This eventually brought about the terrible Civil War with the Federal Northern States, which broke out in 1861 as Abraham Lincoln became President. Meanwhile, theatres were springing up in all major towns and live entertainment was brought to outlying communities by showboats and, eventually, by the network of railroads.
The Music Halls	From the mid-1850s onwards, theatre entrepreneurs in Britain began to build ever more splendid theatres to cater for the entertainment needs of the growing middle classes. These 'respectable' venues had their origins in the raucous and boozy atmosphere of the simpler performance spaces of earlier years where audiences could come to listen to popular songs. By the 1870s, the **music hall** had reached its zenith and remained an essential part of the life of British towns and cities until the First World War. Thereafter it was rivalled by the cinema, but, even today, there are some beautifully preserved and restored music halls and frequent attempts to reproduce the particular kind of magic they represented. The nature of a music hall has been summarised by the actor Simon Callow: 'it was a unique mix of social comment, sexual innuendo, musical brilliance, physical poetry and visual spectacle. It celebrated the grotesque, the defiant, the carnival; above all it was about personality and the give and take between stage and stalls' (*Guardian*, 15 September 2012). Music hall 'acts' became legends, often known by their most celebrated songs, their catchphrases or their extraordinary appearance. They were admired by all sections of society and they laid the foundations of what became 'variety' entertainment. A music hall combined the arts of singing, dancing, acting, circus skills and stand-up comedy and created a dynamic need for performers to engage with their audience.

Political and social events to be noted	**Music halls** developed in Britain at a time of rapidly increasing urbanisation and industrialisation. Tens of thousands of people moved from the country into towns and cities, and the development of the omnibus and the railways enabled audiences to come in from the suburbs to the newly built theatres and places of entertainment. The ability to create wealth from manufacturing and trade and some developments in education led to the emergence of the 'middle class' with time and money for leisure and pleasure. At the same time, there was desperate poverty among the working classes, but if workers were able to gain a small wage, they were often keen to spend some of their earnings on drink and entertainment as an antidote to otherwise dreary lives. As music hall reached its peak of popularity, Britain was extending its overseas empire so that it became the greatest empire ever known. Queen Victoria, its sovereign, and loyalty to the empire became a frequent topic of the songs and jokes of the period but so, also, did the gradual emergence of a new kind of educated and ambitious woman who challenged the accepted family conventions and taboos.
Vaudeville	**Vaudeville** is a term of French origin, where it describes a form of light entertainment consisting of drama, songs and dances which became popular in the small theatres of Paris in the nineteenth century. However, it was in the United States that vaudeville became most widely recognised as a form of Musical Theatre and the expression is still used today. Vaudeville was really an American version of the British music hall, but with increased sophistication and luxury of theatre buildings from the 1880s onwards and the desire to present 'clean, family' entertainment a distinctive art form was evolved. The heyday of vaudeville was from the mid-1890s to the 1920s (when the 'movies' robbed Vaudeville of its audiences), and its characteristics included clever lighting and technical effects, the idea of 'star billing' with the most popular entertainers being 'top of the bill' and stylish acting, singing and dancing, which combined to produce the most well-loved musical 'numbers' of the day. Some of the 'double acts' were particularly successful and they paved the way for today's TV comedy. Vaudeville was frequently influenced by the stars of British and French variety but tended to avoid risqué material. The stars of vaudeville began to attract the level of financial reward that was later echoed in the movies, and many of their songs remain classic 'standards' for performance today.
Political and social events to be noted	**Vaudeville** developed in the United States to satisfy the needs of a newly affluent and leisured level of society. With the rapid advances in technology and a succession of important inventions, the United States had become the most advanced and wealthy nation on earth, and it was inevitable that some of the wealth and technological know-how would be spent on new forms of entertainment. Towns and cities throughout the USA opened lavishly equipped theatres and provided shows that would suit the slightly prudish tastes of middle-class family audiences. At the same time, many Jewish and Irish immigrants brought great expertise in music, dancing and drama to the American scene and many of the leading composers and writers of Musical Theatre came initially from Vienna and other European cities, where light opera and dance were already firmly

established as forms of entertainment. The involvement of the USA in the First World War (1914–1918) was fairly minimal although the sinking of the liner *Lusitania* by a German submarine off the coast of Ireland resulted in the loss of many American lives and brought about a change in attitude and neutrality. Nevertheless, whereas British and European theatre was decimated for some years by the war, the vaudeville theatre of the USA was only finally defeated by the growing popularity of cinema. Much of what had been developed in the live theatre was then translated onto the silver screen.

Key events in the development of the musical, Broadway musical, 1907–1941: The *Follies* and the arrival of the ballad

In 1907, the Broadway producer Florenz Ziegfeld mounted the first of his lavishly staged and costumed **revues** under the title ***The Ziegfeld Follies***. These shows, which were produced every year until 1931, largely consisted of song and dance numbers performed by a huge chorus of glamorous girls and were supposedly aimed at 'the tired businessman'. However, like many other revues, these *Follies* provided opportunities for relatively unknown writers and composers to have their songs inserted into the show.

Perhaps the most significant composer to benefit from this situation was **Jerome Kern** (1885–1945), who had originally created songs for Broadway shows imported from London. He totally embraced the **dance craze** that infected America just before the First World War, and in 1941 he altered the course of Musical Theatre by adding his song 'They Didn't Believe Me' to the show *The Girl from Utah*, which the impresario Charles Frohman had brought from London. Until this point, the central song of revues had been a **waltz**, but Kern's song was a **ballad**, and that form has remained the centrepiece of any musical ever since.

Questions and research activities

- From the late nineteenth century onwards, there were four major centres for the development of Musical Theatre: **Vienna**, **Paris**, **London** and **New York**. During this period, there was considerable anti-Semitism in Europe, and many Jewish musicians and theatre practitioners decided to start a new life in the USA. Study the names in the relevant first section of the Timeline on p. 103 and identify librettists and composers who obviously have European/Jewish origins.
- View the movie *Follies* and make notes on the costumes, choreography and sung numbers. What do you consider to be the dominant characteristics of these shows?
- Find and learn to sing two ballads by Jerome Kern. Who wrote the lyrics and what was the date of composition?
- What were the dance styles that swept Britain and the USA just before the First World War? Search for archival sound/visual recordings to enhance your research. What music was used to accompany these dances?

1918–1931 London: Wit and 'ragtime'

During this period, another master showman was at work. Charles.B. Cochrane produced a series of very popular revues in London, and these were more sophisticated than the *Follies*. Bringing together the influences of American ragtime music and English wit, such shows as *As You Were* and *London, Paris and New York* enthralled audiences with their glamour, dancing and sparkling dialogue. Although the linking themes of the material were sometimes rather tenuous and slim, Cochrane developed a successful working relationship with Noël Coward, one of the most multi-talented artistes in the theatre of the time, and was responsible for a unique succession of **intimate revues**. Songs from these shows are still widely admired and performed by practitioners in Musical Theatre.

Questions and research activities

- Locate sound recordings of Noël Coward performing some of his songs. How would you describe his technique?
- What is 'ragtime' music? Find recordings or sheet music of ragtime and devise dances that seem appropriate.
- Create you own short stage revue consisting of small scenes, songs and dancing, all linked by a theme.
- Research the life and career of Charles B. Cochrane. What qualities did he bring to the stage of his day?
- Study Noël Coward's *Bitter Sweet* and learn to perform at least one song from this show.

1927 New York: The first, great 'serious' American musical

With music by **Jerome Kern** and the book and lyrics by **Oscar Hammerstein II**, the remarkable stage work *Showboat* was to give a new quality to the musical. Not only was it the first such show to have its roots in recent American history but it also treated the subject matter with great seriousness. Because of this, the production did not open with what had become the predictable chorus of pretty girls: instead, it showed a realistic scene of black workers loading cotton bales. The drama ends unhappily and was the first of many musicals to examine the life of 'show business' itself in a critical and not always flattering way. One of the great songs in this musical is 'Ol' Man River', which became enormously popular, especially when recorded by the famous black bass singer Paul Robeson.

Questions and research activities

- Explore the Timeline and identify where Oscar Hammerstein II was librettist. Who was Oscar Hammerstein I? With whom did Hammerstein II collaborate during his career?
- It is sometimes said that Oscar Hammerstein II invariably wrote about nature, music or love. Identify and learn songs that seem to fit this description.

- Identify at least three important partnerships between composers and librettists in this decade and find examples of their work to add to your portfolio of songs.
- Who appear to be the dominant figures in the development of Musical Theatre during this period? How did other shows develop the idea of dealing with serious issues initiated by *Showboat* in the decade that followed its first productions?

1935–1945 London: A phenomenon

During these years, the Welsh-born and famously handsome **Ivor Novello** established a record that has never been broken. He was the librettist, composer and leading actor for a series of **four successive West End 'hit' shows**. Many of his memorable tunes are still sung by Musical Theatre performers, and his particular brand of glamour and nostalgia typifies the London and New York stage of his day.

Questions and research activities

- *Perchance to Dream* and *King's Rhapsody* were two of the shows that brought Novello his success. What were the most popular ballads in these two works? Learn to sing them and add them to your portfolio of songs.
- Discover the names and content of two other Novello works and research their stage history.
- How did the Second World War interrupt Novello's career and how did he respond to it in song?
- In order to fully appreciate the qualities of Novello's work, you need to understand the fashions and dances of the period. Research these carefully and, if possible, view the movie *Gosford Park* (2001, screenplay by Julian Fellowes) in which the character of Ivor Novello appears.
- What do you think might be the advantages and disadvantages of starring in your own show?

Broadway: The start of the Golden Age

Although much of the world was still embroiled in the Second World War, a new and optimistic musical opened on Broadway in New York. *Oklahoma!*, with music by **Richard Rodgers** and book and lyrics by **Oscar Hammerstein II**, was not predicted to be a success by the critics. Like *Showboat* before it, this show challenged the normal expectations: 'no legs, no jokes, no hope', muttered one critic. It was, in fact, well into the production that any chorus appeared on stage, and then it was a group of cowboys!

However, *Oklahoma!* defied all gloomy predictions and not only became the longest running musical in history up to that point but also established Rodgers and Hammerstein (both of whom had previously worked with other collaborators) as arguably the most successful creative partnership in the world of Musical Theatre. Another remarkable and groundbreaking feature of *Oklahoma!* was the **choreography** of **Agnes de Mille**, who had come from a background of classical and modern ballet. The dancing formed an integral part of the mood and storyline and established **choreography** as being of **equal importance with the other theatre art forms** in Musical Theatre. Following on from *Oklahoma!*, Rodgers and Hammerstein almost monopolised the Musical Theatre on both sides of the Atlantic with the stage and screen versions of *Carousel, South Pacific, The King and I* and *The Sound of Music*, each of which appeared to be more popular than its predecessor and all containing songs that remain very popular today.

The 'Golden Age of musical comedy', during which the American musical totally dominated the Western theatre, is generally considered to have spanned 1943–1968. During this period, musicals such as Lerner and Loewe's *My Fair Lady* and *Camelot* suggested a feeling of confidence and order but the seeds of considerable change had already been sown.

Questions and research activities

- Identify the musicals of Rodgers and Hammerstein during the period 1940–1960 by consulting the Timeline. Why do you think that Rodgers and Hammerstein set their musicals in many different parts of the world?
- Which musicals from this period achieved the longest runs in performance?
- How did the musicals with scores by Kurt Weill contrast with those of Rodgers and Hammerstein?
- Find and learn to sing ballads, character songs and duets from the period and explain why they have remained so popular.
- What are likely to be the main ingredients of a typical musical taken from the Golden Age?
- Which shows from this period were based on plays by Shakespeare and George Bernard Shaw?

The 1950s: Rock and pop

The **1950s** saw the rapid development of the **'pop' music industry** aimed specifically at a youthful audience and bringing its 'stars' fame and financial rewards through records, films and TV shows. There was an explosion of energy in films and recordings with the new and daring **rock 'n' roll** music. Popular 'hit' songs from stage musicals also became part of this phenomenon, and some leading performers in musicals subsequently became known through their recordings, DVDs and TV appearances. It was inevitable that the world of **rock music** and the sense of a growing **'youth culture'** would influence the development of the musical.

In **1957**, the major classical composer **Leonard Bernstein** combined his talents with **Arthur Laurents** (book) and **Stephen Sondheim** (lyrics) to create the musical *West Side Story*: a retelling of the story of Romeo and Juliet set in gangland New York. The production and subsequent film version were directed by the **choreographer Jerome Robbins**, who exploited the jazz/rock rhythms of the score and the violence and pathos of gang/racial rivalry to show a world of violence, hope and loss of hope which had begun to infect inner-city youth in the post-war years. Performed by and exploring the lives of exclusively young people, *West Side Story* energised and **popularised dance** to generations of teenagers. Initially, the show received a hostile reception, and a sense of shock accompanied its first performances. This was the first time that a musical had openly expressed dissatisfaction with American society and had appeared to advocate disrespect for authority.

Questions and research activities

- Investigate the following world events from the 1950s: the Suez Crisis, the Hungarian uprising, the Campaign for Nuclear Disarmament. How do you think that these affected and influenced the growth of music and dance styles that challenged convention?
- How do you account for the continuing popularity of *The Sound of Music*? Which do you consider to be its most memorable moments and songs?
- How would you explain the enormous contrast between the qualities of *The Boyfriend*, *The Threepenny Opera* and *My Fair Lady*?
- Explore the various moments when song replaces dialogue and soliloquy in *West Side Story*. Add some of these to your portfolio of performance pieces. How does the spoken word become song at key moments in the musical?
- What was happening in the world of dance in New York during the 1950s and 1960s?

The 1960s and early 1970s: A unique talent, protest, censorship

Following his success with the lyrics of *West Side Story*, **Stephen Sondheim** emerged as one of the most prodigious talents on Broadway, writing the book, lyrics and music of a sequence of remarkable shows. However, in 1968, a very different kind of musical opened on Broadway and quickly transferred to London. This was **the rock musical *Hair*** by Galt MacDermot, Gerome Ragni and James Rado. Written in the shadow of America's catastrophic military involvement in Vietnam that led to the deaths of thousands of young American soldiers and Vietnamese soldiers and civilians, the show presented a rebellious world of protest, anti-establishment attitudes, drugs, youth culture and 'hippie' lifestyles. With its loud amplified music, popular dance and unconventional dress and anti-war sentiments, it challenged the optimistic world view of many previous musicals and the values of the theatre establishment.

In order for *Hair* to be produced in London, another very significant development had to take place. This was the abolition of the Office of the Lord Chamberlain, which for many hundreds of years had exercised censorship over all productions presented on the British stage. Until **1968**, **nudity** or the **representation of God or Christ on stage** had been forbidden by law, but with the removal of these restrictions it became possible for *Hair* and a number of other shows with nude scenes and the musical ***Godspell*** by Stephen Schwartz about the life of Jesus to be seen on the London stage.

The **abolition of stage censorship** in Britain also indirectly brought about a significant shift in the transatlantic traffic in musicals. The young British composer **Andrew Lloyd Webber** and his librettist **Tim Rice** had written a rock musical show for schools based on a biblical story – ***Joseph and the Amazing Technicolor Dreamcoat*** – and by so doing not only created one of the most influential writing partnerships in the history of Musical Theatre but also introduced generations of young performers and audiences to the excitement of the rock musical. The brilliant pastiche, witty lyrics and memorable melodies of *Joseph* remain as popular today as when they were written. But it was Lloyd Webber and Rice's *Jesus Christ Superstar* that exploited the new stage possibilities of the figure of Christ and the clever launching of the most famous song in the show as a recording prior to the stage production which enabled this and several subsequent musicals by these writers to dominate the world stage for some years.

This period, particularly when we view it in retrospect, was also characterised by much more liberal attitudes to sex and to the use of drugs, and these factors are evident in many of the musicals.

Questions and research activities

- Consult the Timeline and identify all the works by Stephen Sondheim: then read his autobiography, *Finishing the Hat.*
- Identify a number of musicals written during this period based on 'real-life' situations, 'real people' or well-known books.
- How does the use of rock music change the nature of the stage musical?
- Select two musicals by Lloyd Webber and Rice and examine their structure. When is spoken language used and how is singing used to replace dialogue?
- Identify at least three musicals from this period which exploit particular cultural situations.

The 1970s and 1980s: New choreography, backstage musicals, ensemble shows and the 'triple threat'

During this period, there were marked developments in the way that musicals were staged and conceived. In the USA, the stage and movie versions of a series of musicals – *Cabaret, Pippin, Dancin', Sweet Charity, All That Jazz* and *Chicago*, all directed and choreographed by **Bob Fosse** – showed a new, raunchy and raw dance style based on contemporary dance and jazz dance. This fitted the subject matter of showgirls, pimps, prostitutes and gangsters and, along with **Michael Bennett's** *A Chorus Line*, tended to focus on the lives, agonies, ambitions and realities of performers themselves. In many such shows, the 'chorus' became the central character, and the simple, sparsely decorated staging of levels and a largely bare stage threw those performers and their lives into relief. In the UK, the dominance of a production company headed by Andrew Lloyd Webber continued with two of its most successful shows: *Evita* and, somewhat surprisingly, *Cats*, based on poems by **T. S. Eliot** and using an ensemble style of presentation and highly energetic and all-pervading choreography by **Gillian Lynne**.

As a result of some of the growing tendencies for musicals to demand that the performers could all sing, dance and act, we see significant changes in the training that potential cast members would undertake. It now became almost essential for performers in musicals to be what came to be known as '**the triple threat**', with highly developed skills that enabled them to respond to the demands of modern production. This idea had been particularly popularised by the movie *Flashdance* and the TV series, movie and stage show *Fame*.

The Musical Theatre was rapidly becoming an arena in which all aspects of the human condition could be explored. Musicals like *Miss Saigon* and the remarkable *Les Misérables* (which is still running in London nearly 30 years after its opening) brought a new seriousness to the art form, and it is significant that, in London, both the Royal National Theatre and the Royal Shakespeare Company turned their attention to the production of musicals.

Questions and research activities

- What impression do you gain of life in the theatre from the musicals *Sweet Charity* and *A Chorus Line?* Study the lyrics of songs from these shows very carefully.
- How would you describe the dance styles introduced by Bob Fosse?
- Find scenes from the musicals of this period that seem to demand equal skill in dance, acting and singing.
- What is the historical background to *Miss Saigon* and how is the show related to the opera *Madame Butterfly*?
- The period we have been discussing was one of industrial unrest, the height of the Cold War and the growing sense of dissatisfaction with authority on both sides of the Atlantic. The British Prime Minister Margaret Thatcher (with her famous pronouncement 'There's no such thing as society') and US President Ronald Reagan encouraged individual wealth creation in the hope that some of this would 'trickle down' to more needy people. With the collapse of many traditional industries and, what now seems, a self-centred and ruthless approach to economics, there was a marked change in the spirit of the age. How are these factors reflected in the musicals of the period?

The 1990s: The musical as global commodity, nostalgia and high technology

Nothing significant happens 'overnight' in the theatre but during this period, as we have seen in the opening sentence of this chapter, we can recognise the culmination of the total dominance of the West End and Broadway stages by the musical. You are likely to see *Cats*, *Evita*, *Miss Saigon* or the Disney-generated *The Lion King* in any major city with a large enough theatre, and they will be versions of the same production. Backed up with sophisticated sound and light systems, these productions may well make the reputation of young 'triple threat' performers but will also attract major stars of stage and screen. This does not prevent a host of new musicals being created, and some will run for many years whilst others will quickly close. Particularly popular are shows which celebrate the life and music of recording artistes such as Elvis Presley or Buddy Holly or the songs of Abba and the styles, fashions and dance of a previous generation, so that an increasingly middle-aged or even elderly audience will patronise the performances whilst a younger generation will be excited by shows that seem to speak of the issues in their lives.

Questions and research activities

- Name some musicals that celebrate the years of rock 'n' roll.
- What has been the effect of the involvement of the Disney empire in the development of the musical?
- Which musicals are based on the songs of well-known performers?
- Research and list as many new musicals as possible created during the 1990s. Which of these was a subsequent success?
- Name three major librettists and three major composers active during this period. Learn a song from each of them and include them in your portfolio.

2000 onwards: Celebrity, revivals, cultural diversity and 'anyone can make it'

With the new millennium there was a sense of optimism in the West but the terrible events of '9/11', the subsequent wars in Iraq and Afghanistan and the financial meltdown in the banking system quickly established a more sombre mood. There was a realisation that, for a large proportion of the world's population, the cultural attitudes and expectations represented by the glamour of the musical were unacceptable whereas it also became realistic to extend the scope of the musical to such diverse concepts as 'Bollywood' and the dance of Black South Africans. Musicals such as *Bombay Dreams*, *Strictly Bollywood* and *Stomp* brought a refreshing vitality to a theatre that seemed increasingly to rely on revivals. Using the ever-growing number of TV talent shows, the Lloyd Webber empire embarked on searches for new 'triple threat' talents to take the lead in *The Sound of Music*, *The Wizard of Oz*, *Oliver!* or *Joseph and the Amazing Technicolor Dreamcoat* (all musicals with a strong 'feel-good' factor), and the emotional journeys of the contestants became public entertainment. At the same time, there was an upsurge in musicals, such as *Billy Elliot* or *The Full Monty*, which suggested that anyone with persistence could be catapulted into stardom. Interestingly, these two musicals had originally been made popular as movies, and there are several other examples from this period of this reversal of what was the norm in earlier years. The mainstream of Musical Theatre and pantomime in the twenty-first century appears to have sold out to the cult of media-generated 'celebrity'. It is likely that the 'stars' of stage shows may be from sport, TV 'reality shows' or TV soaps or even politics.

However, alongside the many lavish revivals, many of which may be a reaction to the gloomy world news, the twenty-first century has spawned a multiplicity of new work in fringe and off-Broadway theatres. It seems as if any topic, book, tradition or event can be the subject for a musical, and writers and composers have drawn upon the collapsing traditional boundaries between dance, music and acting and the use of exciting new 'performance spaces' to create a vibrant Musical Theatre scene.

Remarkable advances in digital technology have enabled producers to create stunning musical and visual landscapes both in huge public ceremonies or in intimate theatre spaces. Musical scores can be sent across the world and it is possible for musicals to be created by writers and performers who never meet.

Performances can be accessed on YouTube and backing tracks can replace live musicians.

Questions and research activities

- Conduct your own survey of the productions currently playing in London, New York or any major city near where you live. What proportion of the shows are musicals and how many of these are 'revivals'?
- What are some of the current issues being addressed in musicals?
- Find songs from new and original musicals being offered in 'fringe' or 'off-Broadway' theatres and add them to your portfolio.
- How have advances in technology affected the development of the musical?
- How do you account for the increasing popularity of Musical Theatre as an art form?
- What is your opinion of the value of TV talent shows? Do they contribute valuably to raising standards of performance in Musical Theatre?
- Fill in any musicals you have encountered that are missing from the Timeline below.
- At the time of writing, the musical *Chicago* had just overtaken *Les Misérables* as the third longest running show in the history of Broadway. *Cats* was second and *Phantom of the Opera* the longest running, with, to date, 10,300 performances. Which are the longest running musicals in the West End? What do these statistics tell us about the domination of the world stage in musicals?

Musical Theatre: A Timeline

1728–1929

Year	Title	Composer	Lyricist
1728	*The Beggar's Opera*	John Gay	
1866	*The Black Crook*	Various	
1891	*Robin Hood*	Reginald de Koven	Harry B. Smith
1906	*The Red Mill*	Victor Herbert	Henry Blossom
1907	*The Merry Widow*	Franz Lehar	Adrian Rose
1910	*Naughty Marietta*	Victor Herbert	Rida Johnson Young
1913	*Sweethearts*	Victor Herbert	Robert B. Smith
1917	*Maytime*	Sigmund Romberg	Rida Johnson, Cyrus Wood
1919	*Irene*	Harry Tierney, Charles Gaynor, Wally Harper, Harry Carroll, Fred Fisher, Otis Clements	Joe McCarthy, Charles Gaynor, Harry Tierney, Jack Lloyd
1924	*The Student Prince*	Sigmund Romberg	Dorothy Donnelly
1924	*Rose-Marie*	Rudolf Friml and Herbert Stothart	Otto Harbach, Oscar Hammerstein II

(Continued)

1925	*No, No, Nanette*	Vincent Youmans	Irving Caesar and Otto Harbach
1925	*Sunny*	Jerome Kern	Otto Harbach, Oscar Hammerstein II
1925	*The Vagabond King*	Rudolf Friml	Brian Hooker
1926	*Countess Maritza*	Emmerich Kálmán	Harry B. Smith
1926	*The Desert Song*	Sigmund Romberg	Otto Harbach, Oscar Hammerstein II, Frank Mandel
1926	*Oh, Kay!*	George Gershwin	Ira Gershwin
1927	*Hit the Deck*	Vincent Youmans	Clifford Grey and Leo Rubin
1927	*Show Boat*	Jerome Kern	Oscar Hammerstein II, P. G. Wodehouse
1928	*The New Moon*	Sigmund Romberg	Oscar Hammerstein II, Frank Mandel, Laurence Schwab
1929	*Bitter Sweet*	Noël Coward	

1930s

Year	Title	Composer	Lyricist
1930	*Girl Crazy*	George Gershwin	Ira Gershwin
1930	*Strike Up the Band*	George Gershwin	Ira Gershwin
1932	*Music in the Air*	Jerome Kern	Oscar Hammerstein II
1932	*Of Thee I Sing*	George Gershwin	Ira Gershwin
1933	*Rberta*	Jerome Kern	Otto Harbach
1935	*Porgy and Bess*	George Gershwin	DuBose Heyward, Ira Gershwin
1936	*On Your Toes*	Richard Rodgers	Lorenz Hart
1937	*Babes in Arms*	Richard Rodgers	Lorenz Hart
1937	*Pins and Needles*	Harold Rome	
1938	*Boys from Syracuse*	Richard Rodgers	Oscar Hammerstein II
1938	*The Cradle Will Rock*	Marc Blitzstein	
1938	*Knickerbocker Holiday*	Kurt Weill	Maxwell Anderson

1940s

Year	Title	Composer	Lyricist
1940	*Pal Joey*	Richard Rodgers	Loren Hart
1941	*Best Foot Forward*	Hugh Martin and Ralph Blane	
1941	*Lady in the Dark*	Kurt Weill	Ira Gershwin

1943	*Oklahoma!*	Richard Rodgers	Oscar Hammerstein II
1944	*On the Town*	Leonard Bernstein	Betty Comden, Adolph Green
1944	*Song of Norway*	Edvard Grieg	Robert Wright, George Forrest
1945	*Carousel*	Richard Rodgers	Oscar Hammerstein II
1946	*Annie Get Your Gun*	Irving Berlin	
1946	*Beggar's Holiday*	Duke Ellington	
1947	*Allegro*	Richard Rodgers	Oscar Hammerstein II
1947	*Finian's Rainbow*	Burton Lane	E. Y. Harburg
1947	*Street Scene*	Kurt Weill	Langston Hughes, Elmer Rice
1948	*Kiss Me, Kate*	Cole Porter	
1948	*Where's Charley?*	Frank Loesser	
1949	*Lost in the Stars*	Kurt Weill	Maxwell Anderson
1949	*Gentlemen Prefer Blondes*	Jule Styne	Leo Robin
1949	*South Pacific*	Richard Rodgers	Oscar Hammerstein II

1950s

Year	Title	Composer	Lyricist
1950	*Call Me Madam*	Irving Berlin	
1950	*Guys and Dolls*	Frank Loesser	
1951	*The King and I*	Richard Rodgers	Oscar Hammerstein II
1951	*Paint Your Wagon*	Frederick Loewe	Alan Jay Lerner
1952	*Wish You Were Here*	Harold Rome	
1953	*Can-Can*	Cole Porter	
1953	*Kismet*	Robert Wright and George Forrest	
1953	*Me and Juliet*	Richard Rodgers	Oscar Hammerstein II
1953	*Wonderful Town*	Leonard Bernstein	Betty Comden, Adolph Green
1954	*The Boyfriend*	Sandy Wilson	
1954	*The Golden Apple*	Jerome Moross	John Latouche
1954	*The Pajama Game*	Richard Adler and Jerry Ross	
1955	*Damn Yankees*	Richard Adler and Jerry Ross	
1955	*Pipe Dream*	Richard Rodgers	Oscar Hammerstein II
1955	*Silk Stockings*	Cole Porter	
1955	*Plain and Fancy*	Albert Hague	Arnold Horwitt
1956	*Candide*	Leonard Bernstein	Richard Wilbur
1956	*The Most Happy Fella*	Frank Loesser	

(Continued)

1956	*My Fair Lady*	Frederick Loewe	Alan Jay Lerner
1957	*Cinderella*	Richard Rodgers	Oscar Hammerstein II
1957	*New Girl in Town*	Robert Merrill	
1957	*West Side Story*	Leonard Bernstein	Stephen Sondheim
1958	*Flower Drum Song*	Richard Rodgers	Oscar Hammerstein II
1959	*Fiorello!*	Jerry Bock	Sheldon Harnick
1959	*Redhead*	Albert Hague	Dorothy Fields
1959	*Gypsy*	Jule Styne	Stephen Sondheim
1959	*Little Mary Sunshine*	Rick Besoyan	
1959	*Once Upon a Mattress*	Mary Rodgers	Marshall Barer
1959	*The Sound of Music*	Richard Rodgers	Oscar Hammerstein II
1959	*Take Me Along*	Bob Merrill	
1959	*The Threepenny Opera*	Kurt Weill	Marc Blitzstein

1960s

Year	Title	Composer	Lyricist
1960	*Bye Bye Birdie*	Charles Strouse	Lee Adams
1960	*Do, Re, Mi*	Jule Styne	Betty Comden, Adolph Green
1960	*The Fantastiks*	Harvey Schmidt	Tom Jones
1960	*The Unsinkable Molly Brown*	Meredith Willson	
1961	*How to Succeed in Business without Really Trying*	Frank Loesser	
1961	*The Music Man*	Meredith Willson	
1962	*A Funny Thing Happened on the Way to the Forum*	Stephen Sondheim	
1962	*Little Me*	Carolyn Leigh and Cy Coleman	
1962	*No Strings*	Richard Rodgers	
1962	*Stop the World – I Want to Get Off*	Lesley Bricusse and Anthony Newley	
1963	*Half a Sixpence*	David Heneker	
1963	*Oliver!*	Lionel Bart	
1963	*110 in the Shade*	Harvey Schmidt	Tom Jones
1963	*She Loves Me*	Jerry Bock	Sheldon Harnick
1964	*Anyone Can Whistle*	Stephen Sondheim	
1964	*Fiddler on the Roof*	Jerry Bock	Sheldon Harnick
1964	*Funny Girl*	Jule Styne	Bob Merrill

1964	*Hello Dolly*	Jerry Herman	
1964	*Golden Boy*	Charles Strouse	Lee Adams
1965	*Do I Hear a Waltz?*	Richard Rodgers	Stephen Sondheim
1965	*Man of La Mancha*	Mitch Leigh	Joe Darion
1965	*The Roar of the Greasepaint – The Smell of the Crowd*	Lesley Bricusse and Anthony Newley	
1965	*Sweet Charity*	Cy Coleman	Dorothy Fields
1965	*Flora the Red Menace*	John Kander	Fred Ebb
1966	*Cabaret*	John Kander	Fred Ebb
1966	*I Do! I Do!*	Harvey Schmidt	Tom Jones
1966	*Mame*	Jerry Herman	
1966	*The Apple Tree*	Jerry Bock	Sheldon Harnick
1967	*You're a Good Man, Charlie Brown*	Clark Gesner	
1968	*Hair*	Galt MacDermot	Gerome Ragni, James Rado
1968	*Promises, Promises*	Burt Bacharach	Hal David
1968	*Jacques Brel Is Alive and Well and Living in Paris*	Jacques Brel	Eric Blau, Mort Shuman
1968	*Your Own Thing*	Hal Lester and Danny Apolinar	
1968	*Zorba*	John Kander	Fred Ebb
1969	*Joseph and the Amazing Technicolor Dreamcoat*	Andrew Lloyd Webber	Tim Rice
1969	*1776*	Sherman Edwards	

1970s

Year	Title	Composer	Lyricist
1970	*Applause*	Chares Strouse	Lee Adams
1970	*Company*	Stephen Sondheim	
1970	*Two by Two*	Richard Rodgers	Martin Charnin
1971	*Follies*	Stephen Sondheim	
1971	*Godspell*	Stephen Schwartz	Plus add music and lyrics by Jay Hamburger, Peggy Gordon
1971	*Jesus Christ Superstar*	Andrew Lloyd Webber	Tim Rice
1971	*Two Gentlemen of Verona*	Galt MacDermot	John Guare
1972	*Grease*	Jim Jacobs and Warren Casey	
1972	*Pippin*	Stephen Schwartz	

(Continued)

1972	*Sugar*	Jule Styne	Bob Merrill
1973	*Dear World*	Jerry Herman	
1973	*Gigi*	Frederick Loewe	Alan Jay Lerner
1973	*A Little Night Music*	Stephen Sondheim	
1974	*Mack and Mabel*	Jerry Herman	
1975	*Chicago*	John Kander	Fred Ebb
1975	*A Chorus Line*	Marvin Hamlisch	Edward Kleban
1975	*Shenandoah*	Gary Geld	Peter Udell
1975	*The Wiz*	Charlie Smalls	
1976	*The Baker's Wife*	Stephen Schwartz	
1976	*Pacific Overtures*	Stephen Sondheim	
1976	*The Robber Bridegroom*	Alfred Uhry	Robert Waldman
1977	*Annie*	Charles Strouse	Martin Charnin
1977	*I Love My Wife*	Cy Coleman	Michael Stewart
1977	*Starting Here, Starting Now*	David Shire	Richard Maltby, Jr
1977	*The Act*	John Kander	Fred Ebb
1978	*Ain't Misbehavin*	'Fats' Waller	Hoagy Carmichael
1978	*On The Twentieth Century*	Cy Coleman	Betty Comden, Adolph Green
1978	*I'm Getting My Act Together and Taking It on the Road*	Nancy Ford	Gretchen Cryer
1978	*Working*	Stephen Schwartz, Micki Grant, Craig Carnelia, James Taylor, Graciela Daniele, Matt Landers, Susan Birkhead, Mary Rodgers	
1979	*Evita*	Andrew Lloyd Webber	Tim Rice
1979	*Peter Pan*	Mark Charlap and Jule Styne	Carolyn Leigh, Betty Comden and Adolph Green
1979	*Sweeney Todd*	Stephen Sondheim	
1979	*In Trousers*	William Finn	
1979	*They're Playing Our Song*	Marvin Hamlisch	Carole Bayer Sager

1980s

Year	Title	Composer	Lyricist
1980	*Barnum*	Cy Coleman	Michael Stewart
1980	*Forty-Second Street*	Harry Warren	Al Dubin
1980	*The Life and Adventures of Nicholas Nickelby*	Stephen Oliver	

1981	*Dreamgirls*	Henry Krieger	Tom Eyen
1981	*March of the Falsettos*	William Finn	
1981	*Merrily We Roll Along*	Stephen Sondheim	
1981	*Woman of the Year*	John Kander	Fred Ebb
1981	*Cats*	Andrew Lloyd Webber	T. S. Eliot
1982	*Little Shop of Horrors*	Alan Menken	Howard Ashman
1982	*Nine*	Maury Yeston	
1983	*La Cage aux Folles*	Jerry Herman	
1983	*Tap Dance Kid*	Henry Krieger	Robert Lorick
1983	*Abbacadabra*	Benny Andersson and Bjorn Ulvaeus	Alain Boublil, Daniel Boublil
1983	*Blondel*	Stephen Oliver	Tim Rice
1983	*Blood Brothers*	Willy Russell	
1984	*Baby*	David Shire	Richard Maltby, Jr
1984	*The Rink*	John Kander	Fred Ebb
1984	*Sunday in the Park with George*	Stephen Sondheim	
1985	*Nunsense*	Dan Goggin	
1985	*Les Misérables*	Claude-Michel Schönberg	Alain Boublil
1986	*Jerry's Girls*	Jerry Herman	
1986	*Me and My Girl*	Noel Gay	L.Arthur Rose, Douglas Furber
1987	*Into the Woods*	Stephen Sondheim	
1987	*The Mystery of Edwin Drood*	Rupert Holmes	
1988	*Chess*	Benny Andersson and Bjorn Ulvaeus	Tim Rice
1988	*Romance/Romance*	Keith Herrmann	Barry Harman
1989	*City of Angels*	Cy Coleman	David Zippel
1989	*Closer Than Ever*	David Shire	Richard Maltby, Jr

1990s

Year	Title	Composer	Lyricist
1990	*Assassins*	Stehen Sondheim	
1990	*Falsettoland*	William Finn	
1990	*Once on This Island*	Stephen Flaherty	Lynn Ahrens
1990	*Aspects of Love*	Andrew Lloyd Webber	Don Black and Charles Hart
1991	*Crazy for You*	George and Ira Gershwin	
1991	*Five Guys Named Moe*	Louis Jordan, arranged by Clarke Peters	

(Continued)

1991	*Grand Hotel*	Robert Wright, George Forrest and Maury Yeston	
1991	*Phantom*	Maury Yeston	
1991	*The Secret Garden*	Lucy Simon	Marsha Norman
1991	*The World Goes 'Round*	John Kander	Fred Ebb
1991	*Children of Eden*	Stephen Schwartz	
1993	*Forever Plaid*	Composers and lyricists from the 1950s	
1993	*The Goodbye Girl*	Marvin Hamlisch	David Zippel
1993	*Kiss of the Spider Woman*	John Kander	Fred Ebb
1993	*My Favourite Year*	Stephen Flaherty	Lynn Ahrens
1993	*Tommy*	Pete Townshend Add. music and lyrics: John Entwistle and Keith Moon	
1993	*The Will Rogers Follies*	Cy Coleman	Carolyn Leigh
1993	*Elegies for Angels, Punks and Raging Queens*	Janet Hood and Bill Russell	
1993	*Honk*	George Stiles	Anthony Drewe
1994	*Passion*	Stephen Sondheim	
1996	*Floyd Collins*	Adam Guettel	
1997	*Jekyll & Hyde*	Frank Wildhorn	Leslie Bricusse
1998	*A New Brain*	William Finn	
1999	*The Civil War*	Frank Wildhorn	Jack Murphy
1999	*The Lion King*	Elton John	Tim Rice

2000s

Year	Title	Composer	Lyricist
2000	*Aida*	Elton John	Tim Rice
2000	*The Beautiful Game*	Andrew Lloyd Webber	Ben Elton
2000	*The Full Monty*	David Yazbek	
2001	*Bat Boy*	Laurence O'Keefe	
2002	*Bombay Dreams*	A. R. Rahman	Don Black
2003	*Avenue Q*	Robert Lopez and Jeff Marx	
2003	*Bounce – Road Show 2008*	Stephen Sondheim	
2003	*Jerry Springer – The Opera*	Richard Thomas	Richard Thomas and Stewart Lee
2003	*The Last Five Years*	Jason Robert Brown	

2004	*Billy Elliot*	Elton John	
2004	*Chitty Chitty Bang Bang*	Richard and Robert Sherman	
2005	*The 25th Annual Putnam County Spelling Bee*	William Finn	
2005	*Acorn Antiques*	Victoria Wood	
2005	*The Color Purple*	Brenda Russell, Allee Willis and Stephen Bray	
2005	*The Light in the Piazza*	Adam Guettel	
2006	*Lestat: The Musical*	Elton John	Tim Rice
2007	*Curtains*	John Kander	Fred Ebb
2007	*Legally Blonde*	Nell Benjamin and Laurence O'Keefe	
2007	*Lord of the Rings*	A. R. Rahman and Värttinä	
2006	*The Drowsy Chaperone*	Lisa Lambert and Greg Morrison	
2008	*13*	Jason Robert Brown	

Carry on with this list and keep an accurate record of all new writing for Musical Theatre that you have heard about or seen

2010s ...

Year	Title	Composer	Lyricist
2010	*Love Story*	Howard Goodall	Stephen Clark
2010	*Love Never Dies*	Andrew Lloyd Webber	Glenn Slater
2010	*The Addams Family*	Andrew Lippa	
2011	*The Book of Mormon*	Robert Lopez, Trey Parker and Matt Stone	
2012	*Daddy Long Legs*	Paul Gordon	
2012	*Sweet Smell of Success*	Marvin Hamlisch	John Guare

(Continued)

Glossary of Studio Terms

Glossary of useful terms most likely to be used in the teaching studio/rehearsal room/theatre

A cappella – (music) unaccompanied singing

Accel./accelerando – (music) gradually getting faster

Accidental – chromatic alterations to pitch using sharps, flats, naturals and double sharps and double flats

Adagio – (music) at ease, slowly

Ad lib – free style and in appropriate time to the needs of the situation

Allargando – (music) broadening, a little slower

Allegro – (music) lively, fast

Anacrusis (or 'pickup' in pop) – the notes at the start of a musical phrase which precede the first downbeat of the next bar – often used to get words such as 'the' out of the way so that the stress falls on the more important word which follows (e.g. 'The rain in Spain stays mainly in the plain')

Andante – (music) at a walking pace, moderate tempo

Anthem – a rousing song identified with a particular group of people or ideology

Aria – operatic word sometimes used to describe a ballad

Arrangement – adding harmony and rhythm to a melody. In musicals a separate dance arranger is common

Aside – lines spoken by the character to the audience – not to be heard by the other characters on stage

ASM (Assistant Stage Manager) – assistant to the deputy stage manager. Usually has responsibility for the props on and off stage. Other roles when and where appropriate

A tempo – (music) in time, return to the main tempo of the piece of music

Atonal – not in any one key or mode

Attacca – (of music) attached, indicates one piece of music is seamlessly attached to the next

Augmentation – augmenting a vocal line would mean stretching it out for longer than its written value

Bar line – vertical line dividing the music into specific number of beats

Ballad – a reflective number examining the inner thoughts and feelings of a character

Bell note – a single note at the start of a song to enable the singer to pitch where no other means are available. This can be *either* an artistic decision *or* one out of necessity depending on the occasion

Biopic – telling someone's life story

Blocking – often the first part of the rehearsal process where the performers are required to record the moves appropriate to the action so that they can be recorded in the prompt copy

Blue note – a note that falls outside of the key signature and is not part of a logical progression in a musical sequence – it deliberately stands out – gives a jazzy feel

Blues third – neither a major third nor a minor third but somewhere in between – often involves a portamento between the two – very common in pop

Book – the structure of a musical, including dialogue

Book musical – a conventional style of musical with spoken word and song (as opposed to through-sung, e.g. *Company*)

Booth singers – off-stage singers whose purpose is to enhance the ensemble singing

Brighter – faster (not louder)

Bridge – often known as the 'release' or 'B' section, containing contrasting music to the 'A' section or main theme

Button – (claptrap) any musical device signalling the end of a song and possibly a planned stopping of the action giving time for audience applause

BVOX – backing vocals

Cadenza – a virtuoso passage for a soloist, often in 'free time' or 'ad lib' – often at the end of a song

Chorus – the repeated part of a song which often clarifies what has been sung about in the more complex verse

Chromatic – involving many notes outside of the key signature

Coda – additional section of music at the end of a song

Codetta – mini coda

Colla voce – flexible tempo, the music follows the singer

Common time – time signature of 4/4

Company Manager – an important role within the theatre production team. Generally to look after the welfare of the cast and to ensure payments are made to cast as and when appropriate; in a resident theatre company more of an administrative role dealing with everyday company issues

Compound time – each beat is subdivided by 3 or 6 instead of the usual 2 or 4

Con – (music) with

Concept musical – a musical where an idea is more important than plot (e.g. *Cats, A Chorus Line* and *Company*)

Counter-melody – a separate thematic idea (even part of another song) sung as counterpoint

Counterpoint – a separate musical line sung between and/or over the main theme

Cresc. – (music) getting louder

Crotchet – otherwise referred to as a quarter note

CS (centrestage) – centre of the performance space

Cue-to-cue – often takes place in a technical sound or lighting rehearsal when the show is run by the cue numbers rather than the action

Curtain calls – company bows at the end of the show. These are usually a rehearsed or an integral part of the play-out music of a musical

Cut time – think 2 half notes (minims) in a bar rather than 4 quarter notes (crotchets)

Da capo – (music) repeat from the start

Dal segno – (music) repeat from the sign

Dal segno al coda – (music) repeat from the sign until instructed to go to the coda

Denouement – resolution

Diegetic – a diegetic song is one that occurs within the world of the characters, i.e. a song a character hears on the radio, or a show within a show. Also called a 'source song' in the film industry (e.g. in the film version of *Cabaret*, all the songs are diegetic. Any numbers that couldn't be made to work in this fashion were cut)

Dim./diminuendo – (music) getting softer

Direct address – when an actor or character addresses the audience rather than the characters on stage. Develops an intimate relationship with the audience (e.g. narrator in *Into the Woods*)

Downbeat – (of music) first beat in the bar – slightly accented

Dramaturg – a theatrical expert who helps to shape and refine the book, music and lyrics

Dry run – a technical run of the show without the actors being present

DS (downstage) – actor's directive to move to the edge of the stage nearest the audience

DSM – Deputy Stage Manager

Dynamics – (music) volume markings

Eighth note – otherwise known as a quaver

Eleven o'clock number – the dramatic turning point of the show, towards the end – often a moment of realisation for the central character. Not all shows have one – some shows have several. Name derived from Broadway in the days when shows started later in the evening, usually 8:00 p.m. – this number would then usually fall somewhere around 11:00 p.m. (e.g. 'What You Own' from *Rent*, 'Back to Before' from *Ragtime*, 'Waltz for Eva and Che' from *Evita*)

Embellishment – see **Ornamentation**

Ensemble – members of an ensemble retain their own individual characters rather than being part of an amorphous chorus line

Ensemble show – a show with no identifiable lead, many characters are of equal importance (e.g. *Into The Woods, Assassins*)

Espress./espressivo – (music) an expressive (emotional) performance is required – the performer is allowed a little flexibility with written note values

Exposition – necessary information that must be communicated to the audience in order for the plot to make sense

Flat – a sign [b] lowering pitch by a semitone

Flies – space above the main performance area where scenery can be raised out of sight from the audience, e.g. fly tower

Foldback – the means by which the orchestra and cast members can hear themselves play or sing in a balanced sound mix

Forte piano/fp – (music) dynamic marking, loud immediately followed by soft

Free time – (of music) no time signature, written notes are only approximate values

Gods – refers to the Upper Circle in the theatre. An exclamation often heard spoken by the director or voice coach . . . '*They won't be able to hear you in the Gods!*'

Grace note – a note of short, indeterminate time value, inserted before another note of fixed time value (also known as Acciaccatura/Appoggiatura). Notated in miniature to distinguish it from a regular note

Half note – otherwise referred to as a minim

Hit point – an accent within the music, often off-the-beat, which multiple singers/musicians must hit at exactly the same time – also called a 'stab'

Incidental music – music used to cover scene changes

Interval – distance between two notes

Introduction – instrumental start to a song. Could be a 'bell' note as well

Iron – a fireproof curtain that can be lowered on stage during the interval of a show

'I Want' song – often the second principal number in a show, where the lead character defines their super-objective (e.g. 'Wouldn't It Be Lovely' from *My Fair Lady* or 'One Song Glory' from *Rent*). All musicals concern a character entering a strange new world, or them finding the world they inhabit being turned upside down. They then require an objective (which they may or may not attain) but the pursuit of this objective drives the plot forward

Key – organisation of tones in a specific order to form a distinct tonality, e.g. major or minor key

Largo – (music) broadly, slowly

Lead sheet – notated vocal line of a song with chord symbols

Legato – smooth singing

Legit – pure vocal quality more suited to light operatic work or Rodgers and Hammerstein ballads

Leitmotif – a musical phrase or idea (and variations upon the same) which follows a character, setting or idea throughout the musical

Lento – (music) slowly

Libretto – the complete text of a musical with song lyrics, dialogue and stage directions. Also referred to as the 'book'

List song – song lyric based upon a list of items, places, ideas, etc. (e.g. 'A Little Priest' from *Sweeney Todd*; 'I've Got a Little List' from *The Mikado*)

LX – lighting cue

Mark – identify a specific place to move on stage

Medley – a piece of music composed from parts of various other pieces

Melisma – changing the pitch of a single syllable while it is being sung

Meno mosso – (music) less movement, slower

Messa di voce – a sustained, sung note that begins softly, gets gradually louder and then dies away again

Meta-musical – a musical in which the characters act as if they know they are in a musical, and which parodies the form (e.g. *Book of Mormon*, *The Producers*)

Metre – pattern of strong and weak beats within a piece of music, or the pattern of stresses within a lyric

Mezza voce – (music) half voice, subdued

Minim – has the value of two crotchets

Modal – (music) not in a conventional major or minor tonality – consistently uses a different hierarchy of notes (a mode). Much folk, rock and pop music falls into this bracket (e.g. if a piece of music looks as though it is in C major, but the 'B' is always flattened, then it is in fact in a mode rather than a major key)

Moderato – (music) at a moderate speed

Modulation – moving from one key signature to another

Molto – (music) very

Monologue – dialogue spoken by one actor alone on the stage

Montage – a musical number allowing rapid progression through a sequence of scenes, often used to show time passing

Mosaic rhyme – where a single word is made to rhyme with a series of other words, e.g. jealous/tell us

Movement Director – as opposed to a choreographer, a movement director works with stylised movement where full dance routines might be inappropriate (e.g. *Les Misérables* contains very little dance but much stylised movement; *Company* would not be considered a dance musical)

Musical Supervisor – supervises the orchestrator, musical director and musicians

Narrative – the story (not to be confused with 'plot')

Natural – a character [natural sign] which cancels a previous musical notation either sharp [#] or flat [b]

Offbeat – deliberately singing behind or in front of the beat – can aid clarity, add interest or be appropriate to the style (e.g. blues)

Off-book – cast often asked to be able to speak dialogue from memory. No books on stage – simplifies the rehearsal process

Orchestration – the art of turning a rehearsal score (usually piano/vocal) into orchestral music

Ornamentation – adding turns, trills, arpeggios, etc., to musical line (e.g. think Mariah Carey!)

Ostinato – a repeated musical pattern

Overture – instrumental music played at the opening of the musical

Pastiche – a tribute to, or 'mickey take' of, a pre-existing style (e.g. 'Pharaoh's Song' from *Joseph and His Amazing Technicolor Dreamcoat*)

Patter – a fast, rhythmic style of singing. A patter song is often a comic solo (e.g. 'I Am the Very Model of a Modern Major General' from *The Pirates of Penzance* or 'Getting Married Today' from *Company*)

Pedal note – a sustained note, usually in the bass, over which the harmony changes

Perfect rhyme – using official rhymes as contained within a rhyming dictionary. This is traditional in theatre to aid clarity, but has been less adhered to in recent years due to amplification and the adoption of popular lyric writing styles

Phrase – a short collection of notes forming a melody

Pickup – see **Anacrusis**

Pit – prepared place usually at front of the stage where the orchestra/band sit and play

Più mosso – (of music) more movement, faster

Plot – the sequence of events which makes up a story or 'narrative'

Poco – (music) little

Poco a poco – (music) little by little (e.g. poco a poco accel. means gradually getting faster)

Point number – a musical number that makes a 'point', often to do with plot or some overarching theme (e.g. 'Take A Letter, Miss Jones' from *Blood Brothers*)

Portamento – pitch bend from one note to another (as opposed to a glissando, where the intermediate intervals are sounded)

Power ballad – highly emotive ballad, often with a driving rhythm

Preprise – a short excerpt from a musical number before the number has been heard in its entirety (e.g. two verses of 'Memory' are sung as the Act 1 finale of *Cats* but we do not hear the full version of this song until near the end of Act 2). n.b. this is a controversial term – not everyone uses it!

Prestissimo – (music) as fast as possible

Presto – (music) very fast

Production number – musical number involving the full company

Prologue – a definite introductory section that opens the musical as a means of explanation to the narrative or style of the musical, e.g. *Something Funny Happened on the Way to the Forum*

Promenade – audiences are able to move around the agreed performance space to see the action from different perspectives

Pros. arch/proscenium arch – often referred to as the 'fourth wall' due to the fact that the two arches on the side of the stage frame the action on stage

Protagonist – the 'leading' actor in the musical/play. Derived from the Greek theatre as being the first actor to speak following the chorus

Quarter note – otherwise referred to as a crotchet

Quasi – (music) imitating, in the style of ...

Quaver – otherwise referred to as an eighth note

Rall./rallentando – (music) gradual slowing down

Recitative/recit – sung material which links, or leads into, principal musical numbers. Often expositional in nature and merely 'functional' in a musical sense. Modern recit tends to reuse themes from elsewhere in the show

Refrain – an old term for the main musical theme of a song

Reprise – reusing musical/lyrical material in a different context to show character/plot development (i.e. not a straight repeat – this would be an encore)

Revue – pre-existing songs linked together by a theme or plot to form a theatrical show

Rhyme scheme – the place where the rhymes contained within a lyric fall – this should be consistent throughout the song (i.e. the rhymes within each verse should be in the same place)

Rhythmic number – an uptempo number, often for chorus or ensemble

Rideout – an instrumental section that concludes the song, often enabling the thought expressed to be continued with action on- or offstage rather than using sung text

Rit./ritenuto – (music) immediately slowing down

Rostrum – raised platform placed on stage to give height to a performance area

Routine – the final structure of a song, including dance breaks, etc.

Rubato – (music) with some flexibility of tempo (i.e. slight speeding up and slowing down as appropriate)

Safety bar (often called a vamp) – bar/s of music which repeat until a specific cue is given

Segue – (music) seamless progression from one section to the next

Sempre – always (keep it the same)

Senza – (music) without

Sforzando/sfz – (music) a dynamic marking indicating a sudden strong accent

Sharp – an accidental [#] that raises a note by a semitone

Showcase – a semi-staged public performance of all or part of a work

Show stop – when a show is stopped due to a technical fault which will impact upon the safety of the performers and production team, or an unruly member of the audience

Sightlines – maintain the action within the view of the audience

Signposting – a hint to the audience (e.g. a leitmotif – see above)

Simile – keep it the same

Sitzprobe – the first rehearsal where the cast meet the orchestra

SL (stage left) – actor's directive to move to the left of the stage facing the audience

Soliloquy – a character talking or singing to themselves (e.g. 'Soliloquy' from *Carousel*), as opposed to a monologue where a character talks/sings to someone else (e.g. 'With One Look' from *Sunset Boulevard*)

Source song – see **Diegetic**

Speed run – a good rehearsal technique when considering aspects of the show or to see how far it has developed. Run-through of an act or the entire show to place the technical features within the production or to give the creative team an opportunity to put in place ideas that need to be developed further. Not aimed to be a polished performance. Entries and exits and rushed-through dialogue are aspects of this work. Performers need to be very secure of dialogue and song cues and to 'pick up' marks quickly

Sprechstimme – half spoken, half sung

SR (stage right) – actor's directive to move to the right of the stage facing the audience

Stab – see 'hit point'

Staccato – short detached

Strophic – repeated musical patterns and phrases but not always the text, e.g. a traditional folk song

Subito – mostly refers to a change in volume *either* quiet to loud *or* loud to quiet

Sub-plot – a secondary series of events forming a story which operates independently of the main plot (although it will bear some relation to the main plot) – this will often act as comic relief (e.g. Herr Schultz and Fraulein Schneider in *Cabaret*)

Syncopation – (music) when the main stresses or accents are offbeat

Tabs – curtains (if relevant). Some modern theatres do not rely on curtains to open and close a show. Lighting effects are often used instead especially in Off West End theatres/pub theatres, etc.

Tacet – (music) an instruction that a performer is silent/not required

Technical rehearsal – often the cast will all be required to attend but this rehearsal is specifically for the stage crew, sound and lighting set, etc. This is another time when the cast must be in complete control of everything rehearsed. This is definitely NOT a rehearsal for the cast!

Tempo giusto – (music) in strict time, e.g. a rock beat

Tempo primo – (of music) a return to the first tempo of the piece

Tenuto – (music) notes to be held for their full value (opposite of staccato)

Top line – notated vocal line

Transposition – changing the key/s of a piece of music to facilitate performance

Tutti – (music) all together

Underscore – music to accompany dialogue

Upbeat – any unaccented beat in the bar (usually 2, 3 and 4 in 4/4 for example). In pop and rock the upbeat is accented on 2 and 4 – this is called a backbeat

Upstage – a derogatory term for an actor who deliberately pulls focus away from the main action of the scene

US (upstage) – actor's directive to move to the upper part of the stage furthest away from the audience

Vamp – see **Safety bar**

Verse – often the section with the most words to be expressed in the song following the introduction. Often encourages the actor-singer to move from speech to singing

Wings – sides of the stage out of sight of the audience

Workshop – a closed session for actors/musicians in order to try out new ideas/work

Geographical Tour of a Vocal Score

Terms in Order of Appearance

Terms and signs	Explanation of terms and signs
Page One	
Title of Song	Said All Of My Goodbyes from the musical *To Death and Glory* http://alexloveless.com/todeathandglory.htm
Music and Lyrics	Indicates writer and composer (Alex Loveless). Good to remember especially if a new musical. They might be in the rehearsal room. Keep alert!
CUE (Antony)	Spoken cue to give warning to the musical director when to begin the music
A	Section A – Verse section. Notice the lyric is more detailed and informative and moves the story forward by giving information and points of interest
grave	Serious mood
Bar line	Vertical line that divides the music score into a series of beats relevant to the top figure of the time signature. This music moves between 4 beats (bar 1) and 3 beats in a bar (bar 21)
Treble clef C D E F G A B C	Indicates the pitch of notes above middle 'C'
Bass clef C D E F G A B C	Indicates the pitch of notes below middle 'C'
𝄴 (4/4)	Time signature: Upper figure **4** = 4 beats in a bar; lower figure **4** = 4 quarter notes (crotchets) in a bar. Solution: 4 crochet beats in a bar
𝄞#	Key signature – E minor – **F** #
adagio	Slow

♩ = c. 69	c. = circa. Approximately 69 crotchets (quarter notes) to be played in a minute
Safety	Repeat bar 1 (can be played many times). Often depends on how long the actor requires to settle into the next part of the musical following the cue spoken by Antony
Repeat bar ‖: :‖	Repeat this section
p	Quietly
Crescendo ———◁	Getting louder
mp	Moderately quiet
Decrescendo ▷———	Getting quieter
CUE (Jonathan)	(Stage cue) Indicates action required by the writers for the opening of the song. These can change within a rehearsal
JONATHAN	Name of character to sing the song
Colla voce	Accompaniment to follow the voice in order that the character is able to control the thoughts. This was experimented with in some detail in the recent film production of *Les Misérables*
Tied note sign	This joins two notes of the same pitch together so that they become longer
Slur	Think of the notes as being carefully joined together and having the feel of a musical 'sigh'
bars 6–7 ———— *mf*	Get louder over 8 beats to moderately loud in bar 8
7	Bar number 7
Poco più mosso	A little more movement
Poco meno mosso	A little less movement
pp	Pianissimo – very quiet
Rall (rallentando)	Slow down
Sprechstimme	Speak at approximate pitch level
Page Two	
8va- - - ⌐	Instruments to sound an octave higher than written

(Continued)

Terms and signs	Explanation of terms and signs
𝄐	Pause. Hold on to the thought as an actor-singer
//	Stop the music and hold the action. Dramatic tension pause
(key signature)	Key signature – E major – **F# C# G# D#**
Molto espressivo	With much expression
andante	Walking pace – steady pace
♩ = 76	76 crotchets (quarter notes) in a minute
Tremolo *tremolo*	Rapid repeated notes like a drum (timpani) roll
ff	Very loud
Sub.	Suddenly
p	Very quiet
>	Accented start on the off beat
Crotchet rest 𝄽	Wait for one beat before singing. This gives emphasis to the expression within the song
𝟯/𝟰	Time signature: Upper figure **3** = 3 beats in a bar; lower figure **4** = crotchet beats (quarter notes). Solution: 3 crochet beats in a bar
Rit. – ritenuto	Slow down immediately
Sub. P – Sub. – subito	Suddenly
♮	Flattens the D sharp to a D natural in the first beat; then C# and G# to C and G natural of bar 28
♯	Return the note to its original pitch G sharp
attacca	Continue straight on (to the next musical number) without any break

Said All Of My Goodbyes

Music and Lyrics by Alex Loveless

Said All Of My Goodbyes

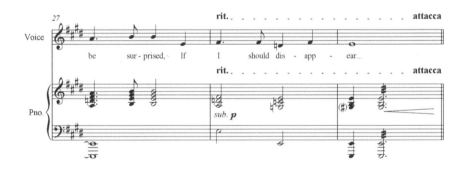

Bibliography

Everett, W. and Laird, P. eds. (2008) *The Cambridge Companion to the Musical,* Cambridge: CUP.

Ganzl, K. (1994) *Encyclopedia of the Musical Theatre,* New York: Schirmer.

Gardyne, J. (2004) *Producing Musicals: A Practical Guide,* London: Crowood Press.

Guernsey, O. ed. (1964) *Playwrights, Lyricists, Composers on Theater,* New York: Dodd, Mead & Co.

Harvard, P. (2013) *Acting through Song,* London: Nick Hern Books.

Henshall, R. (2010) *So You Want to Be in Musicals,* London: Nick Hern Books.

Jasper, T. and Pickering, K. (2010) *Jesus Centre Stage,* Godalming: Highland Books.

Kenrick, J. (2010) *Musical Theatre: A History,* New York: Continuum.

Mackintosh, C. (2010) *The Faber Pocket Guide to Musicals,* London: Faber and Faber.

Pickering, K. (2010) *Key Concepts in Drama and Performance,* Basingstoke: Palgrave Macmillan.

Porter, S. (1997) *The American Musical Theatre,* Studio City, CA: Players Press.

Sondheim, S. (2010) *Finishing the Hat,* London: Virgin Books.

Sunderland, M. and Pickering, K. (2008) *Choreographing the Stage Musical,* Studio City, CA: Players Press.

Tebbutt, G. (2003) *Musical Theatre,* London: Dramatic Lines.

Wheeler, J. and Laughlin, H. (1997) *Assignments in Musical Theatre,* Studio City, CA: Players Press.

Woolford, J. (2013) *How Musicals Work,* London: Nick Hern Books.

Index